Architectural Design 55 3/4-1985

Editorial Offices: 42 Leinster Gardens, London W2 Ø01-402 2141 Subscriptions: 7/8 Holland Street London W8 Ø01-402 2141

EDITOR
Dr Andreas C Papadakis
HOUSE EDITOR: Frank Russell
CONSULTANTS: Catherine Cooke, Dennis Crompton,
Kenneth Frampton, Charles Jencks, Leon Krier, Robert Maxwell, Demetri Porphyrios, Colin Rowe, Derek Walker

Architectural Design Profile 58

REVISION OF THE MODERN

PUBLISHED IN ASSOCIATION WITH  **THE GERMAN ARCHITECTURE MUSEUM**

Guest-edited by Heinrich Klotz

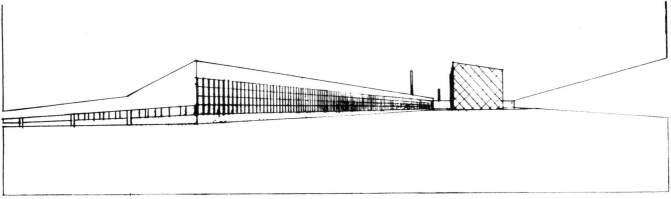

STANLEY TIGERMAN, DOM ADMINISTRATION BUILDING, PERSPECTIVE, 1982

The German Architecture Museum in Frankfurt is the first and only museum devoted exclusively to recording the developing art of architecture. The brainchild of Professor Heinrich Klotz, its Director, the Museum has established a formidable collection of works ranging from drawings and paintings to collages and models. The inaugural exhibition, 'Revision of the Modern', brought together architectural renderings from the last twenty years on the theme of Post-Modernism, and this Profile, prepared in collaboration with the Museum, presents the work of over thirty international architects from the collection. Included are Peter Eisenman, Frank Gehry, Giorgio Grassi, Michael Graves, Haus-Rucker-Co, Hans Hollein, J P Kleihues, Leon and Rob Krier, Richard Meier, Charles Moore, OMA, Aldo Rossi, Massimo Scolari, T G Smith, Ettore Sottsass, Superstudio, Stanley Tigerman, O M Ungers, Robert Venturi and many others. For a full list of contents, see page 3.

Subscription rates (including p & p): Annual rate: UK only £45.00, overseas US$75.00 or sterling equiv. Student rates: UK only £39.50, overseas US$65.00 or sterling equiv. Double issues since 1981: £7.95/US$14.95 plus £1.00/US$2.00 postage and packing. For back issues prior to 1982, please ask for price list. 1986 subscription rates available on request. All subscribers to Architectural Design will receive free copies of Art & Design in 1985 and 1986.
ISSN: 0003-8504

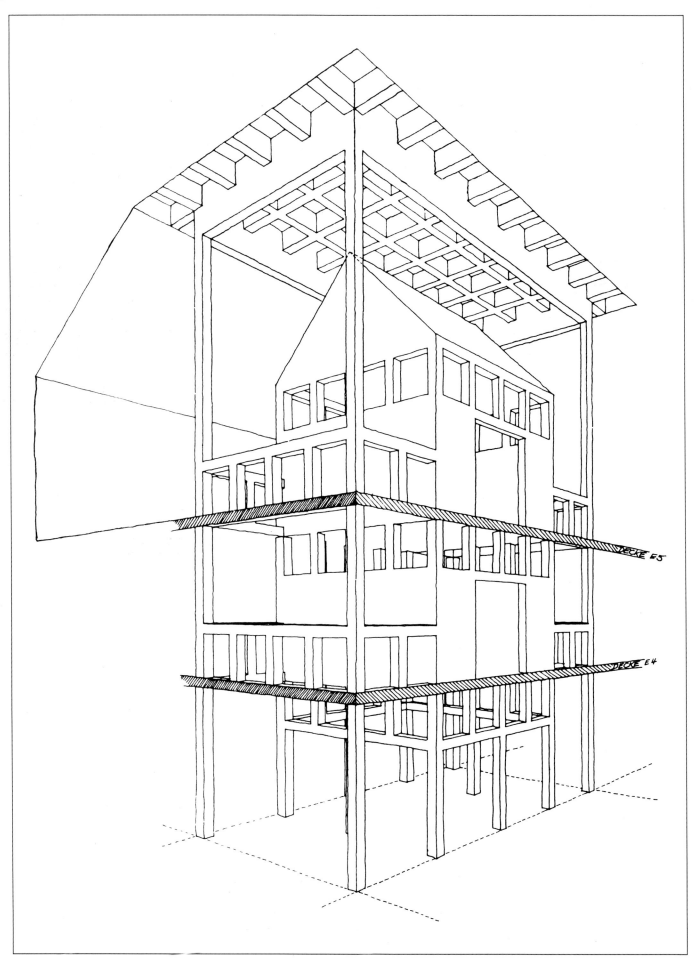

GERMAN ARCHITECTURE MUSEUM, PERSPECTIVE OF THE 'HOUSE WITHIN THE HOUSE'

Architectural Design Profile

REVISION
OF THE
MODERN
THE FRANKFURT ARCHITECTURE MUSEUM COLLECTION

GUEST-EDITED BY HEINRICH KLOTZ

THE FOUNDING OF THE GERMAN ARCHITECTURE MUSEUM 5
Heinrich Klotz

IN THE STEPS OF VASARI 9
Charles Jencks interviews Heinrich Klotz

THE COLLECTION
Raimund Abraham 18; Frank Gehry 20;
Giorgio Grassi 23; Haus-Rucker-Co 24; Helmut Jahn 26;
Josef Paul Kleihues 28; Nils-Ole Lund 31; Gottfried Böhm 33;
Charles Moore 35; Wolf Meyer-Christian 36; Leon Krier 37; Rob Krier 38;
Peter Eisenman 40; Adolfo Natalini 42; Michael Graves 45; Steven Izenour 48;
Office for Metropolitan Architecture 50; Aldo Rossi 52; Massimo Scolari 56;
Thomas Gordon Smith 58; Ettore Sottsass 60; Stanley Tigerman 62;
Chicago Seven 64; Bernhard Schneider 65; John Hejduk 66;
Hans Hollein 68; Oswald Mathias Ungers 72;
Richard Meier 74; Robert Venturi 76;
Mario Botta 78; SITE 79

THE ARCHITECTURE MUSEUM, FRANKFURT 1979-84 81

We are grateful to the German Architecture Museum for providing material for publication; and in particular to Professor Heinrich Klotz for his collaboration and for his many contributions. Our thanks also go to Volker Fischer, Andrea Gleiniger-Neumann and Hans Peter Schwarz, who prepared the majority of the descriptions of the work featured. All photographs are courtesy of the Museum, unless otherwise stated.

First published in Great Britain in 1985 by Architectural Design
AD Editions, 7 Holland Street, London W8

AD Profile 58 is published as part of Architectural Design Volume 55 3/4-1985

Distributed in the United States of America by
St Martin's Press, 175 Fifth Avenue, New York, NY 10010

Library of Congress Catalog Card No 85-61358
ISBN 0-312-67938-6 (USA)
ISBN 0-85670-861-5 (UK)

Printed in Great Britain by Garden House Press, London

THE FOUNDING OF THE GERMAN ARCHITECTURE MUSEUM

GERMAN ARCHITECTURE MUSEUM, INTERIOR

IN SPRING 1969 I WENT TO CHICAGO TO INTERVIEW Mies van der Rohe for my book *Conversations with Architects* (New York 1973). Mies died before I could talk to him, but there was evidence of his work all over his office still. Tucked away in a corner, I found a model of one of those corner-site projects which he used to enjoy so much. I asked Dirk Lohan, the head of the office, what was going to be done with the model and he said that it would be discarded as soon as construction was over. I wanted him to hold onto it for me, because it told the story of how one of Mies van der Rohe's last buildings, the Toronto-Dominion Centre, had evolved. But when I went back to pick it up, it had already found its way onto the rubbish heap. I thought of how much the few remaining models of Renaissance architecture, such as the one of Brunelleschi's dome for Florence Cathedral, meant to us, and how hardly a single original model by a contemporary architect like Mies had survived. And I decided then to start a collection not only of drawings and plans but also of models, as these were the most impressive records of the evolution of a building.

For the next two years, during 1970-71, I taught architectural history at Yale. There I got to know some of the most important American architects: Charles Moore, Philip Johnson and Robert Venturi. While Charles Moore said that Bill Turnbull had many of his models hanging up on the walls of his studio in San Francisco, Robert Venturi admitted that he had thrown out all

his, keeping nothing. At that time no one cared much about sketches and renderings. Indeed it was common practice to throw them out as soon as the plans were complete, thus destroying the evidence of the design process which led to the final building. This attitude changed with the first signs of Post-Modernism around 1970. Here, in fact, drawings were the only way of recording the innovative ideas at the root of the movement, for many of the buildings that Venturi and Moore conceived existed only on paper.

In the early seventies, the new trends in architecture were making themselves felt only slowly in Europe. The movement needed someone to defend it, as became obvious when I chose to discuss Robert Venturi and Charles Moore rather than the standard Mies van der Rohe and Walter Gropius in *Architecture in Contradiction* (US 1973, Germany 1974). The afterword to the German edition of this book was the first German-language description of Post-Modernism, although it wasn't called such at the time.

When I got back to Germany in 1972 I began looking for people who were interested in setting up an architecture museum that would be not just a national archive of plans but a museum with the explicit aim of exhibiting and collecting international architecture. Right from the start I knew that the chances of setting up a museum would be greater if the debate on architecture could be revived. My first move was to arrange a series of one-week symposia at the International Design Centre in Berlin*. So in 1974 Robert Venturi, Denise Scott Brown and Aldo Rossi came to the city for a week and presented their projects and theories to a wide audience. It was the first time that Venturi and Rossi had met, and although they hadn't thought too highly of each other up till then, they slowly came closer together in Berlin. Denise Scott Brown and Robert Venturi presented their short manifesto 'Functionalism Yes, But . . .', and Aldo Rossi surprised people by asserting that the much maligned Classicist Stalinallee in Berlin provided a higher quality of living than any of the new Modernist housing blocks. It caused quite a stir in his audience, but the German architectural press took no notice.

One year later, in 1975, we held a ten-day workshop at the same place with Vittorio Gregotti, Oswald Mathias Ungers, Alison Smithson, Gottfried Böhm and Charles Moore. The theme was 'Integral Building', a concept which surprisingly was not widely discussed at that time. The visiting architects were confronted with the concrete task of developing infill buildings for the partially destroyed Kreuzberg district of Berlin. Their proposals were then put to Berlin architects in public discussions and even the head of the office responsible for the preservation of the city's monuments took part. This workshop prepared the way for the International Building Exhibition in Berlin.

Although these meetings proved very fruitful, I found little support for my proposal to found an architecture museum where this type of symposium and workshop could take place, making it a centre for the exchange of ideas and not just a repository for collected items and archives.

At this time, it seemed that I would never succeed in setting up a museum that would make Post-Modernism known to the public, but I still wanted to support the movement in any way I could. And in fact, the small, almost medieval town of Marburg where I lived was to provide the first opportunity for Post-Modernism to prove itself in Germany. In 1976 Charles Moore, James Stirling and Oswald Mathias Ungers were invited to tackle three separate tasks that centred around the problem of binding new construction to old cities (*New Construction in the City*, 1978). One of the qualities of Post-Modern architecture is that it allows 'pure geometric forms under the light' to relate to the existing environment. The restoration of the old quarter of Marburg was not just a question of retaining the historical monuments, but of successfully tying them to the new buildings. The results impressed the planning authorities in nearby Frankfurt enough for them to apply the same policies on a larger scale in their city. The fact that Richard Meier, Joseph Paul Kleihues and Oswald Mathias Ungers now have buildings in Frankfurt owes not a little to the initiative at Marburg.

I met Charles Jencks for the first time at a symposium on architectural history and sociology at Utrecht University in May 1977. Everyone there was concerned with sociological questions, except for Jencks, who was more interested in defining the different trends in current architecture. I used the term 'Classical Modern' in an attempt to describe these trends and Jencks asked me if I thought that Modernism was at an end. 'Yes,' I replied, 'an era is coming to an end, Modernism is no longer Modern.' Jencks seemed extremely pleased and said that apart from him I was the only one thinking such heretical things. In the same year, Jencks published *The Language of Post-Modern Architecture* and I published an essay called 'Back to the Facade' (in *Gestaltung einer Neuen Umwelt*, Lucerne). My position was similar to Charles Jencks', only I didn't have the pleasure of stirring up the whole architectural world with a daring concept like Post-Modernism.

At our first meeting in Utrecht I also spoke to Jencks about setting up an architecture museum. He was immediately responsive and suggested creating an architectural congress similar to CIAM (International Congress of Modern Architecture), a thought he is still pursuing today.

Also in 1977 there was a change in Frankfurt's local government. This gave me another set of politicians to try and sell my idea for a museum to: I'd already tried in Berlin, Stuttgart and Munich. My tactic was to suggest that the new mayor would need a programme for culture and the arts that would give his administration a high profile.

The new administration turned out to be very receptive. Together with Peter Iden, the Features Editor of the *Frankfurter Rundschau*, I convinced Hilmar Hoffmann, the Minister for Science and Culture, to set up not just a single museum for architecture but several cultural institutions. Originally, the intention was to build a huge culture machine housing several museums and facilities in the middle of the city, like the Pompidou Centre in Paris. But it became clear that Frankfurt was not big enough for such a giant institution. Moreover, it was a much better idea, from an urban planning point of view, to spread the museum functions over several buildings rather than concentrate them in just one spot. The most obvious location was the row of handsome, long-unoccupied, nineteenth-century villas along the banks of the River Main. Some of these villas had already fallen into disrepair and there was a danger that some speculator might sweep them away and build highrises in their place. So the Frankfurt City Council acted quickly: the Museum of Arts and Crafts was extended (Richard Meier, New York), the Carmelite Monastery was converted into the Museum of Pre- and Proto-History (Joseph Paul Kleihues, Berlin), the Rothschild Palace became the Museum of Jewish Culture (Ante von Kostelac, Bensheim), one of the villas was enlarged to serve as the German Film Museum (Helge Bofinger, Wiesbaden), and the one right next to it became the German Architecture Museum (Oswald Mathias Ungers, Cologne). So far three of the museums – the Museum of Arts and Crafts, the German Film Museum and the German Architecture Museum – have been built. The others are still under construction, but should be finished soon.

This would never have been achieved without the rare and great fortune of having, in Frankfurt, a group of intelligent and incorrupt politicians working regardless of party differences towards a common goal. Hilmar Hoffmann and Erhard Haverkampf, the two Social Democrat representatives on the city council, joined together with Walter Wallmann, the Christian Democrat Mayor, to make our seemingly utopian plan the keystone of Frankfurt's cultural policy. There was, however, sharp opposition to our plan from the Liberals and main body of Social Democrats, who saw it as a conservative programme promoting bourgeois values. Our response was that in a society with increasing leisure time, museums would not remain a bourgeois institution for long, but would reach out instead to people in all levels of society. And this is, in fact, what happened. The German Film Museum has attracted a lot of young people and has the highest number of visitors overall. But the German Architecture Museum also managed to draw almost 100,000 visitors in just four months with its opening exhibition, *Revision of the Modern*, which was launched on June 2nd, 1984. It is our belief that cultural commitment need not conflict with social commitment.

THE MUSEUM'S COLLECTION OF PLANS AND THE RE-EVALUATION OF THE ARCHITECTURAL DRAWING

The German Architecture Museum has all the usual facilities such as slide and photo archives. In addition, its library contains first editions of important works of architectural theory from Leon Battista Alberti's *Ten Books on Architecture* onwards. The magazine section has the most important international periodicals. There is also a video and film library with important footage documenting contemporary trends and the history of architecture in the twentieth century, including *Learning from Las Vegas* by Robert Venturi, Denise Scott Brown and Steven Izenour. However, the Museum's most important possession is undoubtedly its collection of models and plans. Although it was started such a short time ago, it already contains a wealth of material. With original models of important projects undertaken in the last two decades, this collection is probably the most important record of current international architecture.

When I began the collection in 1977, a year before the Museum was actually founded, the conditions were relatively favourable because the public at large hadn't yet become interested in contemporary architectural drawings. While there were a few private collectors in the United States, hardly anyone in Europe took the aesthetics of the drawings seriously. The situation changed dramatically in 1980 when suddenly little galleries selling architectural drawings started popping up all over the place. The architectural drawing was once more acceptable 'salon' material and no longer just a collector's item for an enthusiastic few. In the meantime, prices have risen so steeply that public institutions are finding it hard to keep up. Soon these drawings may become the sole preserve of a handful of private collectors.

Even taking into account fluctuations in fashion and passing crazes, it is clear that the architectural drawing is now a desirable item. As long as building was viewed as a purely technical undertaking and aesthetics played only a peripheral role, architectural drawings were limited to technical working plans. The construction and use of a building were explained by functional, dry information and not by aesthetically pleasing pictures. Presentation drawings for clients were commercial, slick and easy to digest, but like the working drawings, they were strictly utilitarian, and when construction got underway they became superfluous. This kind of approach meant that many drawings and plans were simply discarded. Even if there were still some architects who placed value on the pleasing presentation of their work (such as Paul Rudolph), the quality of the architectural drawing stood out only in those projects where getting the thing built was not a serious consideration, namely, in visions of an architectural utopia. Particularly worth mentioning in this context is the English group Archigram, who gave the world of technology a colourful coating of Pop Art. Around the same time, the Metabolists were at work in Japan, and in Vienna, Hans Hollein and Walter Pichler were developing a kind of utopian poetry of architecture. The utopians were not the only ones breaking away from the pragmatist tradition of the fifties: there were others who tried to suggest a complete, attainable environment in their drawings rather than representing just the building to be constructed.

The situation again changed fundamentally when new intentions became evident in the very form of representation in practical building design. In Europe, two architects in particular were responsible for this change: Aldo Rossi in Milan and Oswald Mathias Ungers in Berlin. In a series of plans made between 1964 and 1965, Ungers and some of his students developed a new style of drawing that consisted only of clean sharp outlines. Even in presentation drawings, the precision of the delineation was paramount. Using the drawings and buildings of Karl Friedrich Schinkel as a model, Ungers achieved very early on a classically elegant sublimation of style. This refined style was then a determinant of European Rationalism. Rob and Leon Krier's early drawings were clearly influenced by Wolf Meyer-Christian, one of Ungers' students. Almost simultaneously, Aldo Rossi was developing a very similar style in Milan, but in his drawings the classical and historical references can be seen even more clearly. Rossi was aided a great deal by his colleague, Giorgio Grassi.

Ungers and Rossi made it possible to talk once again of the *autonomous* architectural drawing. But while they first started this style in the mid sixties, it was not until the late seventies that it gained wider recognition. It is no coincidence that the scorn which the Modernists and Functionalists poured on Post-Modernists was directed first at their style of drawing and its aesthetics. For the older Modernists, the architectural drawing was then still, as it had always been, a means to an end. For the Rationalists, on the other hand, it became a 'picture'. Ungers and Rossi countered the conceptions of postwar Functionalism by going back to the sources of 'Classical Modernism' for arguments against the technocratic architecture of the sixties and seventies. Their drawings crystallised not only the new sensitivity but also the new theory: they became the vehicle for the *new idea* even before any of the buildings they represented was ever built. In fact, it took many years for the argumentation to go beyond the drafting table and become a built fact.

The seventies were a period of rupture in which Rationalism began to assert itself. During this time, the relative independence of architectural drawing led to a new aesthetics which eventually became recognised in its own right. Today, both Rationalism and the new architectural drawing are widely established, so that once again there is a danger of the new style becoming merely the standard style, diluted more and more for everyday use until it is eventually a matter of routine. Right now, however, it seems that there will not be a return to the kind of pragmatism in building that prevailed in the late fifties and sixties, and that architects will be attentive to the drawing for a while yet – at least until the realities of building take the drafting tools out of their hands.

The aim of the Museum has been to compile the most complete collection of plans possible, together with the preliminary drawings for individual projects and, where possible, original models as well. The Museum was able, for example, to acquire the plans for Robert Venturi's first buildings – the Guild House and Vanna Venturi's house – as well as the plans and models for Kresge College and other buildings by Charles Moore. Some of the most important buildings by Aldo Rossi and Giorgio Grassi are documented in full. The Museum also has a large number of plans and drawings by Richard Meier, Peter Eisenman, John Hejduk and Raimund Abraham. It has work by English architects, in particular the Smithsons and Archigram, and naturally German, Dutch and Luxembourg architects, such as O M Ungers, Rem Koolhaas and Rob Krier. France, which at last seems to be coming out of the lethargy it fell into with the death of Le Corbusier, is represented in the collection with important projects by Antoine Grumbach, Fernando Montes and Jean Nouvel.

However, it is not my intention to itemise the Museum's entire collection. I just want to indicate that it has succeeded, bar a few notable exceptions such as James Stirling, to gather together in one easily accessible place in the centre of continental Europe a collection that makes it possible to compare the international architecture of the present. All the material in the collection is to be put on a microfiche catalogue so that the maximum number of people will have access to it. In contrast to other architecture museums, which are defined either regionally or nationally, the German Architecture Museum attempts to provide the basis for an international overview of high quality work. In doing so we are following a long German tradition of absorbing the influences of cultures of different countries and reflecting them back again. The tradition of the international architectural exhibition, in which national boundaries are broken through, is an indication of West Germany's continuing intention to give its culture an international orientation and keep opportunities for cooperation and self-comparison alive.

Translated from the German by Pamela Johnston

*See: 'The Pathos of Functionalism', in *Werk/Archithese*, 3, March 1977

7

GERMAN ARCHITECTURE MUSEUM, MAIN HALL WITH MODEL OF GRAVES' PORTLAND BUILDING (PHOTO T HURSLEY)

IN THE STEPS OF VASARI
Charles Jencks interviews Heinrich Klotz

Photo D Meller Marcoviez

HEINRICH KLOTZ

CJ I wanted to ask you about two related things: the German Architecture Museum itself and its great collection of Post-Modern drawings and models. You thought of this collection in 1969 when you visited the office of Mies van der Rohe and found out they were going to throw away a lot of models, including his last project, the Toronto scheme.

HK Yes, that was my first impulse. I didn't manage to get an interview with Mies because he died, but I think I was the last person who saw him, apart from his family. When he passed away, a whole era went with him, all the signs and symbols of his life. Of course most of his buildings were still standing, but those things he directly worked with were being thrown out, and that depressed me.

CJ So you were acting in a preservative role. Did you see yourself in any other role then? Did you see yourself as an historian, as a collector, or as a museum director?

HK At that time, when I was starting work on my book, *Conversations with Architects*, I actually intended to do interviews with Gropius and Mies and all those famous Modernists, but they died soon after, so I had to go on to Venturi, Moore and others. I felt like Vasari going into the workshops of the architects, going down

to the roots of the information and not relying on second-hand facts. And all these things, not only the interviews but also the models, the drawings and the signs of life of a great architect are first-hand information. I am still not so much a museum director as I am an historian and a critic.

CJ But the motive behind it must have been to preserve something that was disappearing, so in that sense you were like an archaeologist, or an anthropologist studying a society which is dying out. You saw your clientele disappearing. And like Soane collecting the world in order to keep it alive, you're breathing life into contemporary architecture by pulling all of this together.

HK It's very kind of you to see it that way: those should be our intentions. Normally we historians only deal with objects and documents, while actually our first intention should be to make history come alive.

CJ But it could be said that it's slightly nostalgic to do that, to gather past memories. In a sense it is almost like Carl Jung or Lewis Mumford's attempts to reassemble the fragments of Western culture itself.

HK Let me interrupt you. Nietzsche made a wonderful distinction between an historian who is an antiquarian and one who is

9

Photo W Krase

RICHARD MEIER, MUSEUM OF ARTS AND CRAFTS

Photo H Klotz

HELGE BOFINGER, GERMAN FILM MUSEUM

of relevance: the antiquarian is someone who collects historical facts without asking if they have a relationship to the present. Nietzsche said that we should write history *backwards* from the present into the past and I think that's a very good idea because by starting with the present you see more clearly which bits are no longer relevant.

CJ Some people, historians particularly, would say that you then distort the past to fit your present preconceptions. In any case, I see your view as very Romantic and German in that it tries to keep the past alive in the present. In a society where everything of yesterday is 'dead stock', as the fashion people say, you see your role as trying to give value to what tends to be ephemeral.

HK In a 'throw-away' society you get the impression that everything of value is thrown away much too fast. When you see people around you, and even yourself, passing things by, it makes you want to be a Romanticist to try to somehow re-establish that which has been and give value to it.

CJ The Museum obviously has a Romantic origin, but what are your roots? Who do you see as your forebears?

HK Well, Vasari is for me a very important person.

CJ And for me too.

HK I see him as the first *real* art historian: the real historian and critic is the one who goes to the artists and architects whilst they are still alive. The living artists are the best sources of information.

CJ But what about other historians?

HK I feel very attached indeed to German Romanticism, by which I mean Goethe and Hegel as much as Jacob Burckhardt and Nietzsche. But I am most interested in the so-called 'Frankfurt School', in Horkheimer, Adorno, Marcuse and also Block.

CJ What about contemporary historians?

HK Well as an art historian I was very strongly influenced by Panofsky whom I met and admired. Of course, the history of style, as practised by Wölfflin, interests me also.

CJ Actually I too was influenced by Wölfflin and his students such as Gombrich and Giedion.

HK Gombrich is of course a great follower in this tradition, but not as important as Panofsky and Aby Warburg.

CJ Well, I would say Gombrich is as important, but in a different way – more as a cultural and theoretical historian. Without him Kenneth Clark would not have been able to think so broadly.

HK Nikolaus Pevsner is important too although he is of quite a different type. I learned a lot from him about putting it all together, trying to combine style, history and typology. His last book on building types, although fragmentary and almost unknown, is I think one of his important ones.

SETTING UP THE GERMAN ARCHITECTURE MUSEUM

CJ I'd like to ask you about the setting up of the German Architecture Museum because it reflects a unique combination of your personality and that of its architect, OM Ungers.

HK Well, first of all, when you have an idea like that you have to find the right politicians to go along with it . . . And that could only be done by presenting a whole programme of several museums together – we call it the 'Museum Mile'. Since there were these old buildings along the river that the city didn't know what to do with, we gave them new functions as museums. We didn't build one large Pompidou Centre, but dispersed all the functions over all the different existing buildings. That was the major idea.

CJ And how did you have that idea?

HK Well, there were some other people in Frankfurt with whom I discussed this. Peter Iden, a journalist from the *Frankfurter Rundschau*, supported the project, and later became the Director of the Museum of Modern Art in Frankfurt. It was first of all a conservationist idea: we wanted to preserve some very fine historical buildings. At first we didn't even really dare suggest using all those villas as museums. It was too daring, funny and incredible: it couldn't actually happen. Then we got support from a Social Democrat politician, Hilmar Hoffmann, and we all went to the newly elected Christian Democrat mayor, Walter Wallmann, and presented this whole programme to him. And he said: 'We are going to do it'. It was very funny. We drove in a Mercedes up and down the road along the River Main and decided well, this one is going to be the Post Museum, this one is going to be the Ethnological Museum and that one is going to be the Film Museum . . . 'Which one do you want for the Architecture Museum, Heinrich?', they said, and I replied, 'Well, the smallest one'. That was how things happened. It was a bit like a fairy tale.

CJ So, you had a very good idea, but the time was also right, and Frankfurt was right. It wouldn't have happened in any other city.

HK The past six or seven years in Frankfurt have been, I think, *universal* years where everything has come together even as far as international architecture is concerned, and all the different ideas which the International Building Exhibition in Berlin is trying to establish have actually been realised in Frankfurt. We were able to bring in Oswald Mathias Ungers, Josef Paul Kleihues, Richard Meier, Hans Hollein and other architects. It was our initiative to get the best architects from all over the world.

CJ You couldn't have done it in England, or even in America or Japan.

HK Why not?

CJ Because although many people, such as John Harris, may have had similar ideas, the cultural situation hasn't been ripe. In

10

Photo J Winde

GERMAN ARCHITECTURE MUSEUM, RIVERFRONT ELEVATION

GERMAN ARCHITECTURE MUSEUM, INTERIOR

other words, it takes the person with the idea – you – but it also takes the right cultural situation. Because Germany had for twenty years after the war been searching for its identity, it was in a position economically and culturally to do the kind of thing that you were doing. And that is always true when visionary things happen: there is a very happy coincidence between the man with the right idea and the economic and cultural situation . . . No other country – Japan or America – has produced as many museums as Germany. As you've said there's a kind of inflation of museums.

HK Well, museums are not the whole story, of course. There's also the Frankfurt Fair and the reconstruction of Old Frankfurt. There are so many things happening at once.

CJ What's fascinating, thinking also of Berlin and the IBA programme, is the way a certain country suddenly becomes dynamic.

HK There were certain dependencies one cannot deny. First of all there were wonderful people. Even the bureaucrats were wonderful, and that's very strange. I'm very much an enemy of bureaucracy, but in this case the bureaucracy was enlightened and that was a very important factor. Normally in Germany the Social Democrats and the Christian Democrats are enemies. But in Frankfurt the Christian Democrats are liberal and the Social Democrats tend towards compromise. Hilmar Hoffmann and Erhard Haverkampf, the leading Social Democrats, are very conscious about tradition, and that is not typical of socialists. It means you must have something of your counterpart in yourself in order to join forces and establish something new. It's very rare.

CJ But even in Germany it's rare, because political life is so polarised between left and right.

HK Yes. But there was another factor. We had tried the same thing on a very small scale in Marburg.

CJ So was Marburg a kind of base from which you jumped?

HK Yes. Haverkampf, the senator responsible for building and city planning, respected the work we did there and called us to Frankfurt. That was in 1976.

CJ It might be worth mentioning here the sums of money involved. If I understand correctly, your building cost about £2½ or £3½ million; Richard Meier's building alongside it cost some £10 million, the Film Museum cost £6½ million, and Stirling's Gallery in Stuttgart cost £12 million.

HK At last year's rates of exchange those figures are about right.

CJ Yours was the first big architecture museum of the eighties to get off the ground. Since then the International Congress of Architecture Museums has developed, bringing together representatives of museums in Amsterdam, Stockholm, Helsinki,

Moscow, Basle, Breslau, Washington, Montreal and the Museum of Modern Art in New York. Our London example is the RIBA's Heinz Gallery. The French Museum is developing fast, not to mention the Getty. A new genre of architecture museum emerged in the early eighties of which yours was the first large-scale example.

HK Yes. The distinction is important. The old architecture museums were really national archives – of plans, drawings, designs – and for lack of space most of them had almost no possibility to display their material publicly. The major idea behind the type of museum we have established is precisely exhibition. We aim to exhibit architectural documents in order to demonstrate and popularise ideas which are of value to us. At the same time our collection differs from many others in being *international*. On that basis I think the only enterprise really like ours is Phyllis Lambert's Architecture Museum in Montreal. MOMA in New York is international, and it has an architecture department, but it is not an architecture museum.

CJ No, but it does exhibit living architects. So does the Pompidou in Paris. Plainly all these activities relate to yours, but Frankfurt is undeniably the most aggresive and visible example of this new typology. If we look at all this activity in an historical perspective, we are in a position to reassess the role of architectural history, to put architecture socially on a level with art. Whereas you would expect this exhibiting and propagandising from artists, architects are now reasserting their traditional role, and with it are somehow finally coming up the social scale once more.

HK Yes. That has to do with the fact that architects are no longer considered to be only technicians, but are once again being regarded as artists. That means they have to do with fantasy and inventeness of a kind that is quite different from technological inventiveness. It makes them appear broad-minded again. It associates them with a different world and a different way of life.

CJ Do you think that in a certain period, both architects and society went through a definition of architecture as something completely functional and utilitarian?

HK It was that way on the Continent at least, and certainly in Germany.

CJ Where would you draw the boundaries of that period?

HK Between 1955 and 1972 our tastes were rather strongly functional.

CJ So the architect in that period was considered a glorified kind of plumber or electrician?

HK You may say that. Yes. Because he was just supposed to provide a 'service'.

CJ And why do you think that was?

11

ROW OF COURTS

COURTYARD WITH MODELS BY MICHAEL GRAVES

HK I think the architects themselves wanted it that way.

CJ Was it? Or was it more a great cultural misunderstanding?

HK Certainly it had to do with the dividing up of the world into 'culture', on the one hand, and 'civilisation' on the other.

CJ Those are very old, established categories in German thinking, by the way.

HK That's true. In the present period this division took the form of a differentiation between the world of culture and the world of economics. High culture belonged to the artists – and the priests – whereas architects belonged in the world of 'modern civilisation'. The analysis may be characteristically German, but the situation is the same everywhere.

CJ Yes. But what I want to ask you is this: are you putting the blame for it on Modernist ideology, or on the overall cultural situation, or both?

HK Both of course.

CJ And to what degree?

HK Nowadays, when an architect gets involved in designing a world of his fantasy he does not develop a world of High-Tech utopian cities; he develops a world of poetry, a metaphorical world. When we think about the future, we no longer desire an astronaut's world. That's very naive.

CJ Of course in a consumer culture, and in Britain which has tried desperately to be more progressive, the hope of technology expressed by High-Tech still looms large in people's fantasies.

HK That surprises me, because England has a very strong tradition of Post-Modernism.

CJ No.

HK Let us say it has a very strong tradition of historic architecture.

CJ Yes, that's true.

HK And in James Stirling it has one of the greatest architects of our time, and of Post-Modernism.

CJ But he hasn't worked here for many years.

HK It even has an architect like Leon Krier, who decided to live in England because he found an environment he could accept. I do not perceive England as a country of High-Tech architects, although there are famous ones like Foster and Rogers, and of course Cedric Price and Peter Cook.

CJ The worlds of business and computers still see technology as the great white hope of the future. All I mean to say is that while there is a Post-Modern shift going on, there is also something that I have called Late-Modernism which represents a continuity because there the progressivist utopia is still strong.

HK Nevertheless we have to go forward. More than ever we have to believe in new values which extend architecture to something more than a mere fulfilling of technical ideas.

CJ So you see Modernism as conservative and reactionary?

HK I see today's Modernism as exactly that. That's precisely what I wrote about in my book. Our concepts have constantly to be redefined. 'Progressiveness' does not permanently guarantee progress.

CJ I would agree with you.

IS UNGERS A POST-MODERNIST?

CJ Why did you choose Ungers?

HK Well, Ungers is a very important architect who has influenced, through his drawings and concepts, a whole new generation of architects not only in Germany, but also in Italy and to some extent America. Ungers is a very great teacher, but he hadn't been getting commissions.

CJ Why else did you go to Ungers?

HK When I interviewed him for a book on German architecture I suddenly met someone with an opinion about architecture which nobody else had – a kind of humanist opinion. He knew about

12

COURTYARD WITH MODELS BY CHARLES MOORE

INTERIOR DURING THE 'REVISION OF THE MODERN' EXHIBITION

the newest developments around the world but he also knew about the continuity of architectural theory from Alberti to Gropius. He could extend knowledge further back than the Bauhaus . . . I suddenly realised that there was a very strong connection between us, because I thought in those terms too. It was a meeting somehow between lonesome people who recognise each other.

CJ The German Architecture Museum is a good building because it's half you as a client and half him as an architect. In fact, I think it's his best building to date, and I wonder how much of you is in it?

HK He is the architect and the prime mover. He built the building, not me. The role of the client is to stay in constant contact and discuss every detail. This was Ungers' first building in Germany after he came back from the United States. The actual commission was drawn up in 1979. I told him that we had a very narrow little site with a house already on it, so he should surround it all with a large wall and make an introverted museum. And he said, 'Well, it's not only going to be a wall, it's going to be a building because I'm going to cover the wall with a glass roof'. The 'house within the house' was completely Ungers' idea.

CJ I think it's a shame that the interior 'house' doesn't extend outside the roof as originally planned. One thing which has created a controversy in Germany is that it doesn't look very Post-Modern because it has no explicit ornament. It's very white and abstract, and Ungers believes in the 'New Abstraction'.

HK I think the building is not as abstract as Ungers believes. There is very little ornament, but the building is very 'fictitious', as I have defined the word. Fictitious means you create an illusionist world which is not identical to the function that the building fulfils. Besides the function something else has to be there, something aesthetically autonomous, a self-contained world with its own values and its own message.

CJ Many Modern things have been done on that level. I mean Le Corbusier's world or Louis Kahn's or Melnikov's or even Mies van der Rohe's worlds were full of things which were not strictly utilitarian. That's why I don't think 'fiction' is an adequate definition of Post-Modernism.

HK No. 'Fiction' is the core of the definition although you need some more information because you have to find out what *type* of narrative is there. I think that Ungers' building is a highly 'fictitious' building because it has a theme, it has a story. It happens that out of a four-columned space down below, by constant mutations from storey to storey, a building finally grows. That is the story, how the 'house within in the house' comes about. That is not Functional or Modern.

CJ No, but it's Modern in the sense that it believes in the autonomy of architecture and it concentrates on architectural themes . . . Both Ungers and Rossi have been partly in the Modernist and Late-Modern camp. Both of them are part of the New Abstraction, and they both look on extra-architectural things as negative.

HK Well, in my opinion there are different aspects of Post-Modernism, and I think Rossi's and Ungers' way of understanding Post-Modernism, or their architecture (which is not Modern anymore), is a very different way from your way or Venturi's way. You are much more pictorial, you bring in many more values from outside the architectural world. You work with attributions, whereas Rossi and Ungers work with the typology of architecture itself as a narrative, fictitious potential.

CJ In a way, however, it's not so different from Mark Rothko or Jackson Pollock painting the subject of painting. And Mallarmé, who has to be considered *the* Modernist poet, defined Modern poetry as *pure* poetry; poetry about sounds, about the language of writing and speaking. In a way the De Stijl group and Peter Eisenman have also been very conscious, as Modernists, in focusing on the autonomous language itself. In that sense Rossi and

13

Ungers are partly Late-Modern, and my whole critique of what you've done is to obscure these differences both now and in your exhibition, *Revision of the Modern*.

HK From your point of view you are right because you have a very distinct, and rather narrow, definition of Post-Modernism, whereas I widen it out.

CJ I'm sorry that's not true – I widened it out.

HK But I use Post-Modernism in a more general way.

CJ You may do that, but I have listened to Rossi calling himself a Modernist and even denying he's a Post-Modernist. In my writing I have tried to be very general and talk about the whole movement and not exclude people. I am an inclusivist, but I must say that a series of architects from Van Eyck to Stirling to Venturi to Rossi to Ungers have all, at various times in the last five years when I have called them Post-Modernists, denied their Post-Modernism and claimed to be Modernists. And when they do that they are pointing to real continuities with the past which, it seems to me, your typology of 'fiction' obscures. My typology of Late-Modernism makes the distinction clear, and I think one of the problems in your exhibition and theory is that you include people like Richard Meier, who is in no way a Post-Modernist.

HK Well I used him as an opposition to Post-Modernism. I *move out* of Post-Modernism again. I extend the concept so that it becomes clear that Post-Modernism has another aspect to it . . . Meier also 'historicises', he restores early Modernism.

REVISION OF THE MODERN

CJ I want to talk a little bit more about the distortions in your book and exhibition *Revision of the Modern*. First of all your not visiting Japan and seeing the Japanese architects, I think you would admit, is a failing.

HK I think that's a very great loss.

CJ Personally I've tried hard to include the Japanese in the situation, because one is always aware that Westerners are forever keeping people outside the fence.

HK I think there, Charles, you have done a great service. I'm sorry that I don't know Japanese architecture. I only write about architecture after I've seen it. I never write about something which I only have seen in photographs.

CJ Well, there's another distortion regarding the English situation, because Stirling is not in the exhibition. Isn't that caused by the fact that he wouldn't sell you his drawings, or lend them to you?

HK No. I wrote to him and asked him several times if he would take part in the exhibition but he didn't answer. That's the simple fact.

CJ Alright, but I would still criticise you for not noticing that Jeremy Dixon, Terry Farrell and myself have been doing important building in England and elsewhere for the last four years.

HK Except for Thomas Gordon Smith and Steven Izenour we included only the first generation of Post-Modernists.

CJ Yes, but you know perfectly well that I was doing the Garagia Rotunda way back in 1977.

HK I know but I would not consider you as an architect being among the first generation like Venturi, Moore and the others. Our Museum has only 2,000 m² exhibition space and I had to try to get in as many important projects by Post-Modern architects as I could: I made the decision to concentrate on the first generation of primary figures, who started between 1960 and 64.

CJ Can I contradict you? That may have been your intention, but your intention has been slightly deflected by the fact that you were building up a corpus of drawings and models, and what you had in this corpus has influenced your view of history. Within the general level of 'fiction', if we can focus on that, you include a lot of people that I have included in my definition such as Bruce Goff

– people who don't fit into Modernism. And there's a whole tradition of those other people like Soleri and Herbert Green. There are countless people who are just lone-wolves, and who do fictional things.

HK I admit that my book is still fragmentary but that's true of all books on the subject.

CJ That's absolutely right. I wouldn't be saying this if I didn't respect your book. All I'm saying is that it's so good that it ought to be better. You must accept that. I realise you were instrumental in introducing the ideas of Post-Modernism to Germany, not only in your commissioning of Venturi *et al* in 1974, but also in your writings. Your German foreword to *Conversations with Architects* in 1973 was the first to consider many of the key ideas. But as the German Vasari of the movement it seems to me you must not simply base your view on what you have seen. History is not written by world travellers and cannot be, although it must be written from a world viewpoint. Many people have criticised me for not seeing a building and I try and see as many as I can. But if I had to make my personal bank account responsible for writing history I would have given up long ago, because I couldn't.

SYMBOLISM AND POST-MODERNISM

CJ Heinrich, the last bone I have to pick with you is over one impetus of Post-Modernism, that is symbolism and meaning in architecture. In your history I don't think you refer to *Meaning in Architecture* which I edited with George Baird, or any of my other writings with Geoffrey Broadbent. We did an issue of *AA* magazine on meaning in architecture and symbolism and sent copies to Venturi. Then we asked him to write for our subsequent anthologies. In fact Panofsky, Gombrich and all of those people were going to write for us. Semiotics and the history of semiotics in architecture was very strong.

HK I know that *Meaning in Architecture* was a very important book for me too.

CJ In the early seventies before Venturi got into signs and symbols and *Learning from Las Vegas* . . . I'm just saying, I suppose every person has got to blow his own trumpet or else the world doesn't notice.

HK Maybe I should have written a chapter about Charles Jencks and not only one about Robert Venturi. But you know we are in the same boat. We don't always recognise ourselves, we are always commentators. To recognise a critic as the maker of history is not usual. It takes a closer knowledge: in fact I simply didn't know you well enough.

CJ But you know my early work was all symbolism. I've written two anthologies and many articles on meaning in architecture and semiotics and Venturi has picked them up. That is a fact.

HK He's never mentioned it. He doesn't quote them.

CJ He quotes only Alan Colquhoun from *Meaning in Architecture*. I don't want to say that I invented Venturi or anything, but to do historical justice to the idea I have to say that George Baird, in a sense before me, picked up the Italian and French arguments about structuralism and semiology and translated them into architecture in 1966. We wrote a series of articles which were influential and then went to conferences in Italy and made links with the Italian semiologists. That was very important for all of the symbolism of the early seventies and Venturi. And when the history comes to be written . . .

HK Why don't you do that?

CJ Well I have in a very minor way.

HK Why don't you make a strong statement?

CJ I only saw it after I looked at your book and I thought: 'My God, he doesn't know about it and Paul Goldberger doesn't know about it'. Because people read Venturi straight, they don't see where he got these ideas. Your book has been written partly

Photo T Hursley

THE GERMAN ARCHITECTURE MUSEUM BEFORE (BELOW) AND AFTER (ABOVE) RESTORATION

INNER COURTYARD WITH MODELS OF HOUSING IN VIENNA BY ROB KRIER

within a German context and your feeling is that Germany – and Ungers – have been underrated by the outsiders.

HK   Yes. I think so. There was for instance a strong historicising tradition in Germany after the war when our cities were being rebuilt. There are great names like Stephen and Schwarz which are utterly unknown outside Germany. And of course there are other architects like Behnisch who opposed the idea of perfectionism in architecture much earlier than Frank Gehry.

CJ   Surely Hans Scharoun was an alternative?

HK   Scharoun was the architect who opposed rectangular architecture like nobody else: even Aalto learned from him. He's another figure who is not so well-known, but who was very important in the early twenties. There is also a strong Expressionist tradition represented by Gottfried Böhm whom I consider to be one of the most interesting architects practising today. He's a real pluralist whose work comes from Expressionism.

CJ   Is he appreciated now?

HK   In Germany yes, but there is very little knowledge of German architecture and culture in England and America. I think we care more for you than you do for us.

CJ   There's your films and Günter Grass, etc.

HK   That's happened only recently.

CJ   There's an awareness, but I don't think your architecture has been that developed. The explosion of Post-Modernism is this incredible dynamic thing where – boom boom boom – it moves faster that you or I can think. So suddenly in the past four years, due to your efforts and Ungers and Kleihues and luck, Germany has become very important. No one could have predicted that. In 1976 I would never have said it would happen in Germany.

HK   But the architecture in Germany was not as interesting as in America or even in England when Jim Stirling was building there.

CJ   Tell me how Stirling is perceived in Germany.

HK   He is considered to be one of your greatest architects.

CJ   Is he? And the Staatsgalerie in Stuttgart is enjoyed?

HK   Oh yes. Even its opponents are beginning to understand and admire it.

CJ   I think it's a very good building. I don't know if you think that.

HK   I like it.

CJ   It's a building that grows on me.

HK   It's a building that lives on many different levels. It has that wonderful exterior, it has that 'landscape architecture' and it has that great interior. It's so varied that it's actually a constant adventure to be in, on or around it. So I think it's a very important building. I also think that Stirling learned something from Hans Hollein's Mönchengladbach Museum. They worked together in Dusseldorf and I think that Hans Hollein had some impact on Stirling.

CJ   Certainly Hans Hollein told me that he introduced Stirling to Schinkel.

HK   I think it's a wonderful thing that we already have museums by Hollein and Stirling, and I think it will be even better when Richard Meier's building is finished.

CJ   And of course yours pulls it all together as the Vatican, or at least Museum, of Post-Modern Architecture.

16

THE ARCHITECTURE MUSEUM COLLECTION

RAIMUND ABRAHAM

Megabridge, 1965

The *Megastuctures* and *Houses* series demonstrate how Abraham's concept of an architectural utopia changed from the sixties, when he depicted a future dominated by technology, to the seventies, when he represented a rather mythical, poetical world.

The earlier drawing, *Megabridge*, shows a city made up of pipes containing accommodation units and supply installations. Like a giant express train, the structure pushes continually forward – over mountains and rivers, lakes and wastelands. The prototypical landscape and the rounded form of the composition indicate Abraham's desire to make the concept universally valid. The drawing is one of a series, *Megastructures* c 1962-65, which stimulated architectural debate in the sixties.

Nine Houses, Triptych, 1972-76

The later work, the triptych *Nine Houses*, summarises Abraham's work in the seventies. It represents a complete change of approach. Here, the architecture reflects feeling, intuition and fantasy. Archetypes and metaphors of houses are described and individual themes, such as the 'house with curtains' or the 'house with inner shadows', are clearly articulated. The exploded axonometrics and the surrounding obscure landscape show the influence of Walter Pichler's drawing style.

Together with Massimo Scolari, Leon Krier, Hans Dieter Schaal and John Hejduk, whom he influenced, Raimund Abraham is one of the most influential exponents of the theory that drawing a concept is just as valid as building one. 'Architecture must first of all be an idea,

then the idea can be realised. There are several ways of doing this. One way is to make a drawing. I am not saying that the architectural drawing is an intermediate product – something resulting only out of frustration at a lack of building commissions. . . If the drawing really takes shape as a complete architectural idea, then it is an end product'. (Abraham)

With the 'built drawing', the aesthetics of architecture not only recaptures an essential part of its own history (from Piranesi to Boullée), but also comes closer to contemporary art forms such as individual mythologies, concept art and environmental art.

The *Cosmology of the House* borrows elements from the *Nine Houses* such as the path, the waving curtains and the way in which the landscape is depicted.

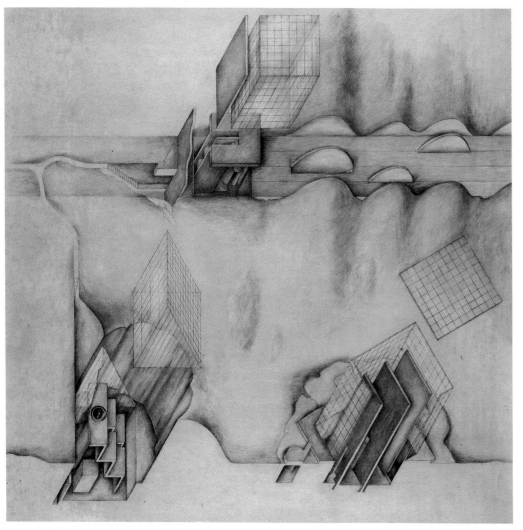
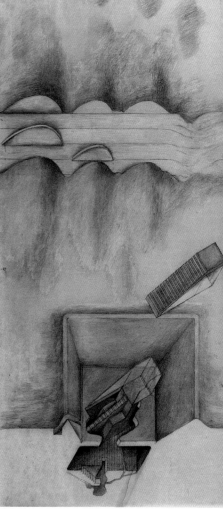

'NINE HOUSES' TRIPTYCH, 1972-76: 1 HOUSE WITH INNER SHADOWS; 2 HOUSE WITH PATH; 3 HOUSE WITH THREE WALLS; 4 HOUSE WITH THREE HOR

'MEGABRIDGE', 1965

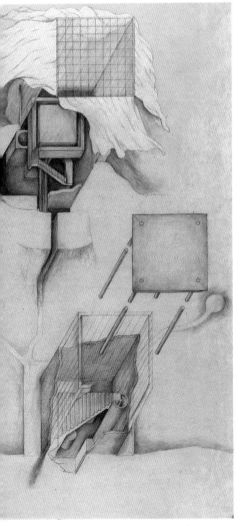

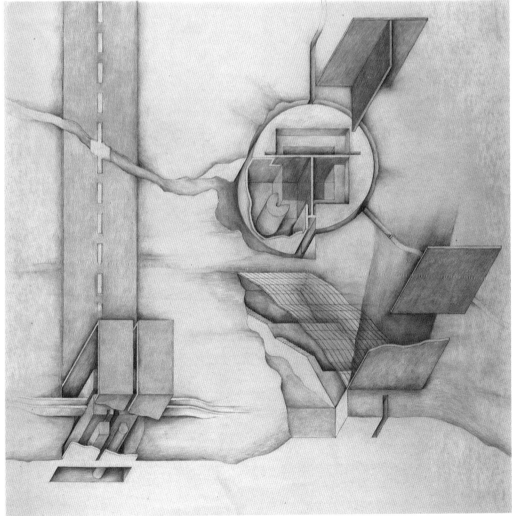

USE WITH CURTAINS; 6 HOUSE WITH FLOWER WALLS; 7 HOUSE WITH STREET; 8 HOUSE WITH THREE ROOMS; 9 HOUSE WITH PERMANENT SHADOWS

19

FRANK GEHRY

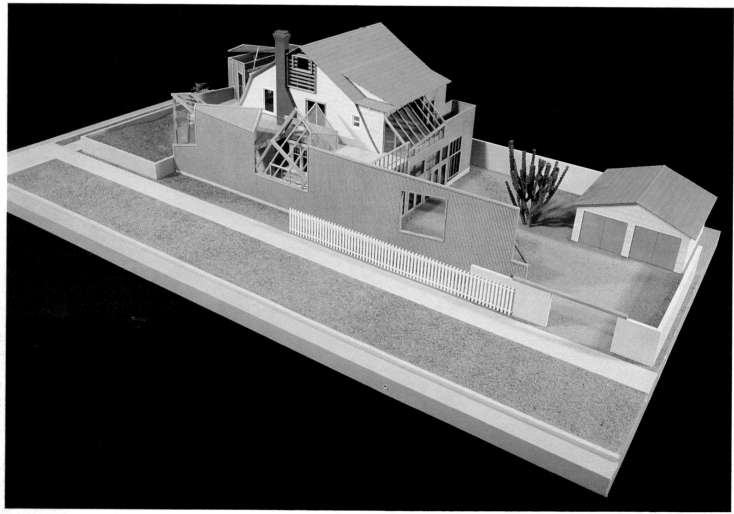

VIEWS OF THE MODEL, FROM THE NORTH (ABOVE), AND THE NORTHEAST (OPPOSITE)

Gehry Residence, Santa Monica, California 1979

This residence in Santa Monica can be read as the manifesto of Frank Gehry's 'non-finite' architecture. The core of the complex is a salmon-pink, hip-roofed house fairly typical of the middle-class neighbourhood where it is located. However, any impression of normality is shattered by the extensions which wrap around the house like a shell. The east, or entrance facade, first strikes the visitor as a temporary hoarding composed of dangerously unstable wire mesh and fragments of corrugated metal. The impression of an 'architecture in progress' is reinforced by the double flight of open stairs leading up to the front door. While one flight corresponds to conventional architectural ex-

perience, the other consists of three slabs of concrete seemingly thrown randomly one on top of the other. Above the stairs, two wooden landings appear to ram the front door back into the facade. The effect of an unfinished, almost mobile architecture is further strengthened by the northeast corner of the building. Here, the corrugated metal is ripped open by a glass cube whose outrageous position suggests that it simply rolled off the roof and landed that way.

The working drawings for this apparent house of cards reveal, however, that it has been thought through to the last detail. It was very much Gehry's deliberate decision to make the house still appear to be under construction even when complete: it was his way of freeing it from what he sees as the procrustean con-

straints imposed on building by bureaucracy and money. In this respect, Gehry's choice of materials is significant. These are, for the most part, amongst the cheapest available on the market, allowing him not only to make a statement about the economics of building but also to highlight the handmade elements in his work.

Gehry's 'non-finite' architecture has been applied not only to his own home but also to museum buildings, such as the Cabrille Museum in San Pedro, to several art galleries and even to a lawyer's office. His attempts to reclaim building as an artistic activity and in doing so save those qualities lost by bureaucratised mass-producers of architecture are not the least reason why his work has met with such acclaim both in the USA and Europe.

20

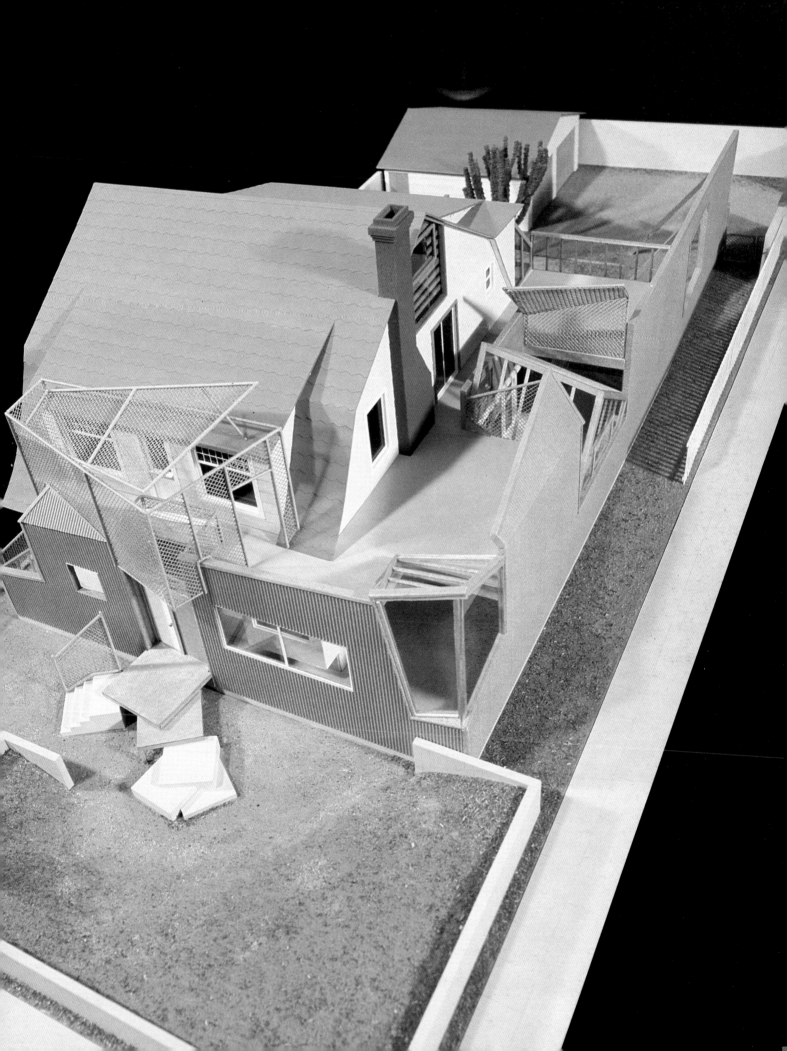

STUDENT RESIDENCE IN CHIETI, VIEW OF STREET

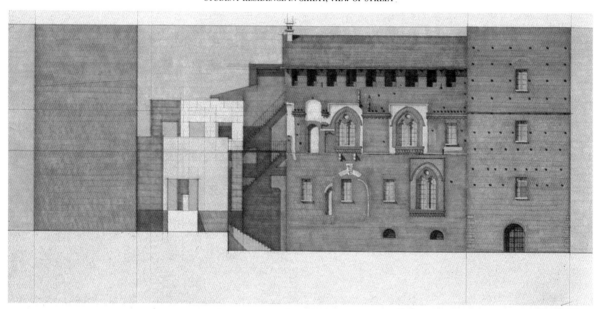

ABBIATEGRASSO, VIEW LOOKING EAST WITH A SECTION OF THE STAIR

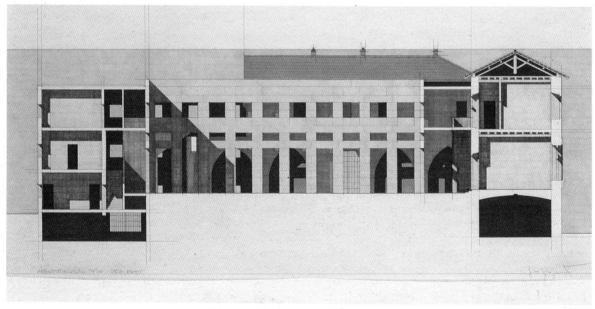

ABBIATEGRASSO, VIEW OF THE COURTYARD LOOKING WEST

GIORGIO GRASSI

U BASILE LABORATORY, PERSPECTIVE OF THE INNER COURTYARD

U Basille Laboratory, Paullo 1968
This factory for the manufacture of experimental apparatus for biological research had to be erected on a small corner site bordered on the north and east by two major roads. Because of the delicacy of the work, it was necessary to seal the complex so that the main entrance was the only opening to the outside. Grassi proposed a U-shaped building with an inner courtyard edged by a colonnade. The building lies on a grassy slope that extends to the end of the site and is interrupted only by the open stairs of the main entrance. The nature of the drawing allows the project to remain a conceptual architecture, one of those 'collective pointers to the future' so important in Grassi's concept of a social utopia.

Project for the Conversion of the Viscount's Castle in Abbiategrasso, Milan 1970
This unbuilt design for the conversion of a former palace into a town hall for the small community of Abbiategrasso, near Milan,

clearly demonstrates Giorgio Grassi's 'image of history'. At the centre of his reflections was not the historic value of this structure – which was in any case unquestionable – but its active meaning in the architecture of the town as a whole. Grassi felt it important to recreate the dominance that the castle had once exercised, though naturally through other means than restoring the Milanese seigniory. He proposed to add a new fourth wing to the castle and new porticos to the inner courtyard which would have risen slightly above the existing cornice line. Grassi's view is that the differences between the old building and any new construction should not be glossed over but retained as a taut contrast: the dialogue between old and new should form the basis of the composition. 'The "old" set next to the "new". Where the "old" remains intact and bears witness to its own history and that of the town. Where the "new" does not give up its own identity, but remains architecture and still stands as a witness to history in the broadest sense.'

Student Residences in Chieti, 1976
Grassi's proposal for student residences in Chieti was the winning entry in a competition in which Aldo Rossi, the 'father' of Italian Rationalism, also took part.

In contrast to Rossi's design, in which individual, almost village-like housing units were grouped around a central community hall, Grassi's proposal was a classically defined 'street' reminiscent, in its overall form, of an eighteenth-century rationalist hierarchy. The entrance halls and staircases are the common typological elements which, in opening onto the street with colonnades, pick up on a characteristic element of urban architecture. The colonnade, as demonstrated also by the projects at Paullo and Abbiategrasso, is something of a trademark of Grassi's architecture. Here, it is combined with the 'street' to recreate an environment typical of public life in Italy since the middle ages, thus counteracting the danger of a student ghetto.

HAUS-RUCKER-CO

'VILLA SUBMARINA'

Nike, **Linz 1979 and Frankfurt 1981**
Haus-Rucker's *Nike* (meaning 'Victory', in Greek) was originally made for the 'Forum Metall Linz' exhibition in 1979 and first soared from the roof of the Linz School of Fine Art.

Haus-Rucker based their work on a very famous Greek sculpture, *Nike of Samothrace*, which now stands at the top of a flight of stairs in the Louvre. Square by square, they transferred a photographic reproduction of Nike onto two perpendicular aluminium panels cut in the same shape as the marble statue. Then they attached the Goddess of Victory to a steel support arm to enable her to soar in the sky with her aluminium wings. Depending on which

way the viewer approaches the work, it can be either a three-dimensional sculpture or a two-dimensional profile. Haus-Rucker's *Nike* both alienates and brings up-to-date the original.

Nike of Linz can be seen as a sarcastic criticism of Classicism, because of the huge enlargement of the original subject and the unusual use of materials. It can also be thought of as a reference to Constructivism, because the metal structures in the work are left visible and the steel support arm bears more than a passing resemblance to elements in El Lissitzky's 'Lenin Tribune' project. It is both of these things and more – an ironic collage of many diverse strains of twentieth-century art, notably Symbolism.

Haus-Rucker's *Nike* is very much a contemporary work. It contradicts all the notions of mass and proportion which generations of painters saw encapsulated in the original *Nike of Samothrace* and brings together technology and poetry, modernity and history, restoration and revolution in a work charged with tension. After being dismantled in Linz, *Nike* found a new home on the Museum Bank in Frankfurt in 1981.

Like *Nike*, the *Villa Submarina* is a comment on Classicism.

Members: Günther Zamp Kelp, Laurids Ortner, Manfred Ortner.

24

'NIKE' ON THE MUSEUM BANK IN FRANKFURT

MODEL OF THE GERMAN ARCHITECTURE MUSEUM, FRANKFURT

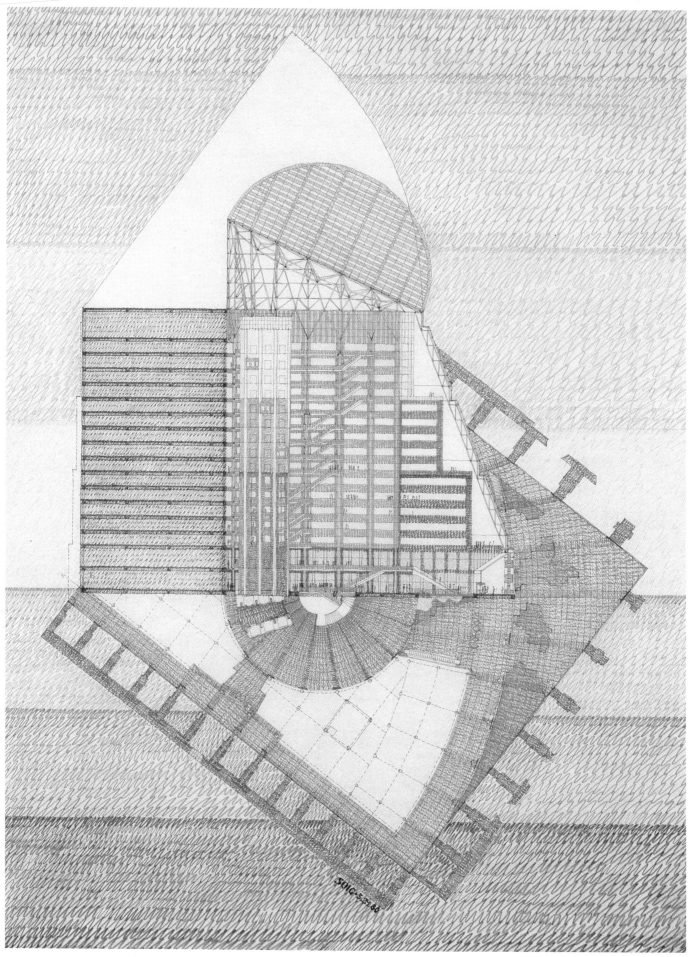

STATE OF ILLINOIS CENTER, CHICAGO, FLOOR PLAN AND SECTION

HELMUT JAHN

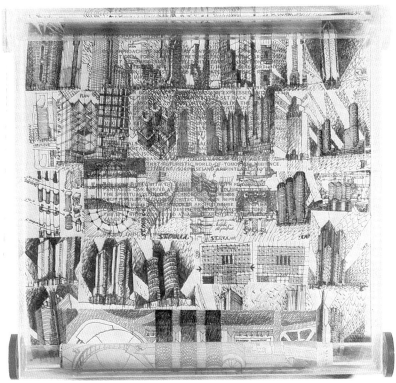

'SKY-SCRAPERS' 1980-81

Sky-Scrapers, 1980-81
This scroll represents an archetypal metropolis of skyscrapers, beginning and ending with a 'manifesto' of types (reproduced below). The sketches demonstrate Jahn's ability to evoke grand and powerful concepts with just a few lines on a small piece of paper. And the originality and spontaneity of these initial thumbnail sketches is often maintained through large presentation drawings.

'Our approach to skyscrapers synthesises an approach to traditional form – which stretches from historic arch-typal to Art Deco/Moderne – coupled with formal invention using modern materials and techniques not in a literal, orthodox duplication, but abstracted to create meaningful references and image.

This effort to create a «historical continuum» inspires us to give our buildings refined bases and expressed entrances, articulate the shaft or progressively set back the building's bulk, and give them definite tops unlike the shaft-like towers of the Modern Style. This «new synthesis» is not of an abstract nature/not of a technological utopia, but a recomposition of all those elements, its interest is in form image and

expression beyond technological determinants, which will shape a building's systems and components along a logical and objective analysis.

These goals are coupled with an almost romantic drive to create fantasies for human use and living. We see those buildings as isolated objects, that are at the same time part of the urban context. Those rays of light act as a theater for that futuristic world-of-tomorrow ambience. They create excitement, surprise and are intended to be people pleasing.

The continuity with the past together with futuristic fantasies can arrive at a temporary settlement between the spiritualistic and technological trends of our age. Such popular machine architecture can represent a genuine synthesis between modern architecture and popular culture, one which was denied to Modern architecture in the twenties, which conceived a machine architecture in advance of technology.'   *Helmut Jahn*

State of Illinois Center, Chicago 1979-84
For this administration building, Jahn chose not an historicising concept but a geometric one, inserting into Chicago's highrise landscape

a segmented, truncated cone, cut off vertically to fit into the existing city grid. At first glance, the scale of the building seems too large for its site: it steps back three times, implying a massive horizontality, before it rises to a flat roof. Green, blue and white opaque bands of windows create varying degrees of transparency and reflection, and order the glass facades. Inside, a rotunda pushes upwards through the height of the building, bringing light to the offices around it and creating an enclosed public space (or inner city atrium of the type common in the United States since Kevin Roche's Ford Foundation Building). The rotunda pushes through the flat roof and terminates in a diagonal cylinder slice reminiscent of the top of a half-opened tin can.

In a structure intended to symbolise the power of the federal state, the combination of basic geometric forms – a 'roofed' cube, a segmented cone and a sliced cylinder – draws the building to monumentality by its negation. In Heinrich Klotz's words, this administration centre is not 'a form that is complete . . . but a fragment that explains itself by the geometry of the buildings and streets immediately around it.'

27

JOSEF PAUL KLEIHUES

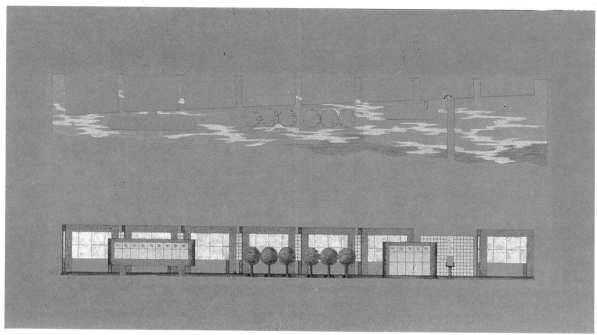

SPRENGEL MUSEUM, HANNOVER

Like Ungers, Kleihues has been concerned with the manipulation of form since the sixties.

Housing and Shopping Centre, Wulfen 1975-81
Wulfen is a new town built in the sixties to house 32,000 people. Although it has a good location in the open countryside, it is still a town without a heart, without an historic centre. To create just such a focal point Kleihues designed an assemblage of three large terraces, each with their own orientation. The terraces are a collage of typological elements such as the passage, colonnade and terrace, given identity by allusions to their historical qualities. Naturally, practical considerations were also taken into account. There is a covered shopping arcade, because it rains almost all the time in Westphalia, a sheltered two-storey colonnade where children may play, and a small look-out with views of the countryside.
Collaborator: Ulrich Falke.

Sprengel Museum Project, Hannover 1972
The arrangement of equal masses and volumes was the determining principle of this competition entry. The design consists of a block of eight cubes – 21m high pavilions of glass, stone and aluminium – with a glazed entrance which

provides access to the diagonal gallery linking all the elements of the composition. In front of the museum block, a surrealist row of 'ball' trees paraphrases the rationalist origins of the design and carry it into the realm of nature.

Kleihues has said that the only credible way of combining historic and modern architecture is to preserve their separate identities, but make them complement each other. His projects for the Ephraim Palais and Solingen archives demonstrate this approach.

Municipal Archives at Gräfrath Cloister, Solingen 1979
The Gräfrath cloister in Solingen has undergone various structural changes since its secularisation in 1803, owing to frequent changes in its use. In the past it has been a farm building, a reformatory and an old people's home. This scheme proposed to preserve the old cloister as a museum for swords and blades (Solingen being the centre for cutlers in W Germany) and house the municipal archives in two new towers nearby. The towers have a common base which is in sympathy with the site, but one tower has an open steel skin and the other a closed stone facade. They represent the dialectic between the sheltered archive rooms and the open work-

spaces where new documents are collected, between the past and the present. On the roof of the steel tower is the representation of a leaf; leaves blowing in the wind symbolising the history of life, and written leaves symbolising the history of the town.
Collaborators: Thomas Barthels, Mirko Baum and Jean Flammang.

Ephraim Palais, Berlin 1979
The Ephraim Palais was demolished in 1936 to make way for a wider road. After the war, however, the numbered stones were discovered in West Berlin and the Senate decided to rebuild the palace for the Jewish community and provide cultural facilities there.

Kleihues' proposal was not only to reconstruct the palace but to add on a new wing which reflected the proportions of the old building and joined with it to create an open courtyard. At the point of juncture, the old and new buildings are held together by a nave-like colonnade which ends in a semi-circular 'choir' – an historical allusion that is ironically voiced as a staircase.
Collaborators: Mirko Baum, Ulrich Falke and Rudolf Hauser.

28

MUNICIPAL ARCHIVES AT GRÄFRATH CLOISTER, SOLINGEN

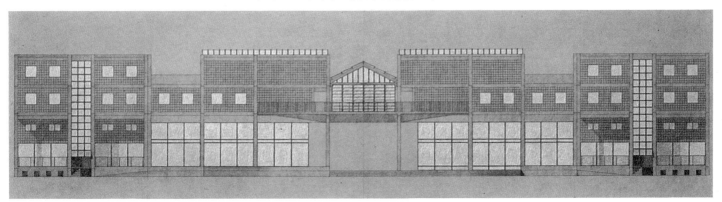

HOUSING AND SHOPPING CENTRE, WULFEN

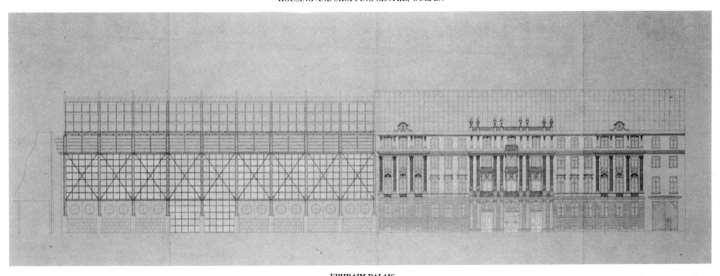

EPHRAIM PALAIS

29

'JAMES STIRLING'S ENGINEERING BUILDING'

'PICNIC IN THE GREY'

NILS-OLE LUND

'SKYSCRAPER ON THE ROCKS'

The Future of Architecture, c 1976-81
Like Ettore Sottsass, Nils-Ole Lund sets visions of ruin against promises of a 'beautiful new world' of Modern architecture. In Lund's collages, the symbols of progress become the symbols of decay. James Stirling's Leicester University Engineering Building is shown as a monumental ruin – not as a building which has aged gracefully, but as a pile of rubble and scrap. In another collage, *Skyscraper on the Rocks*, Lund places the banal symbols of inter-

national night life against the backdrop of a Dutch still-life.

The use of alienation and ironic interpretation to criticise Modern architecture and the belief that technology equals progress has its roots in Pop Art. In 1964 Pol Bury showed the Pan-Am Building cut up into tiny pieces.

Unlike the Italian group Superstudio, whose *Twelve Ideal Cities* series summons up terrifying visions of megastructures running rampant all over the earth, Lund leaves open the possi-

bility of a new start at the end of it all.

Lund also uses the medium of the collage as a metaphor for architecture in general, because it is a combination of differing and separate elements and fragments. By allowing these elements to gradually evolve into a complex whole, and by openly showing the tensions and breaks within the composition, Lund is clearly demonstrating that he is a partisan of Robert Venturi's 1966 manifesto, *Complexity and Contradiction in Architecture*.

31

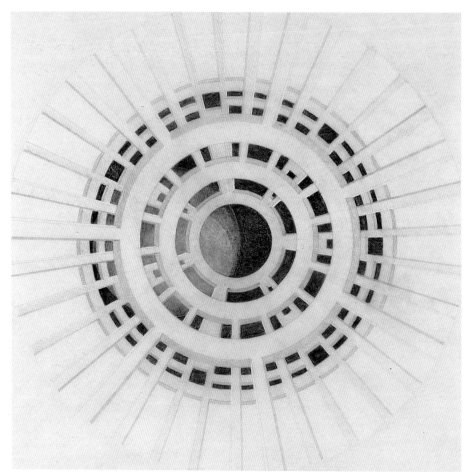

SAARBRÜCKEN CASTLE, DOME

PRACTICE THEATRE AT FOLKWANG SCHOOL, ESSEN, PERSPECTIVE OF THE AUDITORIUM

GOTTFRIED BÖHM

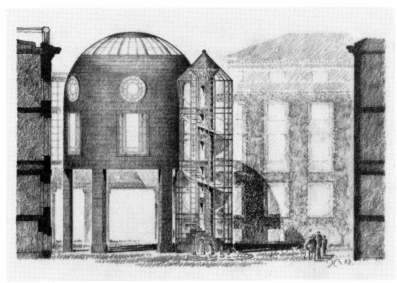

SAARBRÜCKEN CASTLE, VIEW OF THE ENTRANCE PAVILION

Conversion of a Castle in Saarbrücken, 1982
Böhm was given the task of creating a new pavilion within an old castle by Von Stengel that would not only provide accommodation for the parliament of the federal state of Saarland but also reflect the Baroque form of the original building while using light, modern construction materials. With the addition of a new central facade to replace the one destroyed by fire in the nineteenth century, Böhm has restored the outline and axis of the castle. In this project as in so many others, he has proved himself a master at mediating between the old and the new.
Collaborators: Nikolaus Rosini, Krüger-Rieger, Fissabre.

Practice Theatre at the Folkwang School, Essen 1979
Gottfried Böhm is particularly fond of using exposed steel framework in theatres. It is a technique he has applied with great success not only to monumental buildings such as the Stuttgart Opera House and Munich Theatre but also to small-scale projects, such as this practice theatre for a school in Essen. Here the framework creates a pitched roof, which Böhm has suggested covering with a fresco of clouds to emphasise the lightness of the structure and highlight the contrast between technology and nature. Out of this confrontation comes a piece of narrative architecture which makes it possible to forget the 'silence' of bare construction.
Collaborator: Stephan Böhm.

SAARBRÜCKEN CASTLE, VIEW OF THE WHOLE FACADE

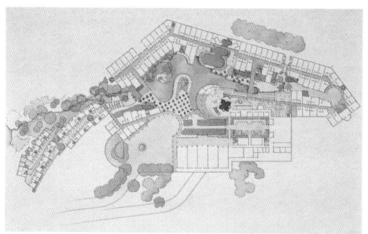

HOTEL IN SAN JUAN CAPISTRANO, CALIFORNIA: ELEVATION (TOP); FLOOR PLAN OF COMPLEX (CENTRE); AXONOMETRIC (BOTTOM)

CHARLES MOORE

PIAZZA D'ITALIA, NEW ORLEANS, MODEL

Piazza d'Italia, New Orleans 1977-78
The Piazza d'Italia was built to give identity to the Italian community in New Orleans. It is a splash of Mediterranean colour and form in an otherwise bleak neighbourhood.

Moore took full advantage of the opportunity to use historicism in this project, as is immediately made obvious by the temple-like entranceway to the plaza. However, he interpreted the historical forms quite freely and ironically. The bases of the fluted columns on the colonnade within are like fragments of an architrave defined as a negative form rather than as a full, plastic detail. Some column capitals are reminiscent of crystalline Art Deco brooches, other capitals are ringed by neon necklaces. Moore himself has talked of a 'Delicatessen order . . . that we thought could resemble sausages hanging in a shop window'. All of these things tie the vocabulary of classical architecture to the present.

The plaza is cut in the shape of a circle containing a graduating series of rings that move from black to white like the graphics of a nearby office building. The rings lead inwards towards a fountain shaped like Italy, with water running down the rivers Po, Arno and Tiber. Moore also wanted to place 'Tiki Torches' at the place on the map where Vesuvius would be, but there wasn't enough water for that. High, cascading forms at one end of the fountain represent the Italian Alps, while at the other end, the island of Sicily marks the centre of the circular plaza and the homeland of most of the Italian community in New Orleans.

The Piazza d'Italia is both a stage set crammed with playful references to Baroque and Renaissance palaces, and an open air meeting place in the Italian *res publica* tradition. It has provided a focal point for an urban quarter which was in danger of becoming a slum.
Collaborators: Urban Innovations Group, Ronald Filson, August Perez, Malcolm Heard, Allen Eskew; Christine Beebe (Colour coordination).

Hotel in San Juan Capistrano, California 1982
This unrealised project was a competition entry for a hotel in San Juan Capistrano, a community whose predominantly Spanish colonial-style architecture bears witness to its past as one of the most important mission towns in North America.

The characteristic feature of Charles Moore's diverse structure is its sympathetic relationship to the landscape around it. The complex's introspection and romantic silhouette give it the appearance of a rather monastic refuge and so link it with the rich tradition of the stone or adobe missions built by the Spanish in California. Moore also responds to the character of the architecture of the region with the village-like arrangement of the complex.

This project demonstrates Moore's love of incorporating water into his architecture. As in the Piazza d'Italia in New Orleans, the centre of this complex is a series of basins and a kind of small lagoon. Bordered by colonnades, these basins recall thermal baths and Roman villas.
Collaborators: John Ruble and Robert Yudell.

35

WOLF MEYER-CHRISTIAN

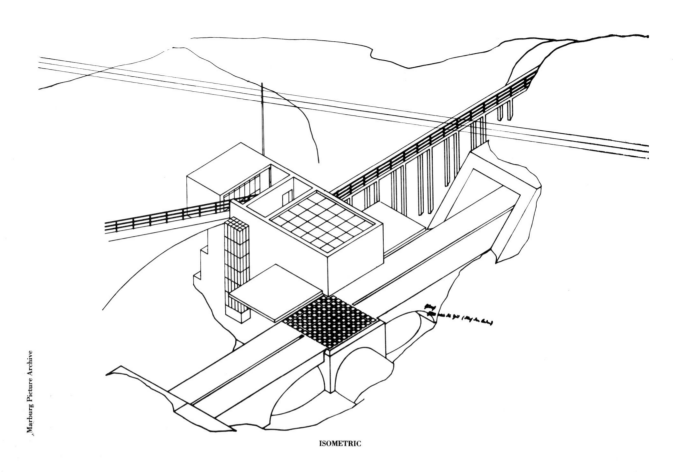

ISOMETRIC

Housing Project, Berlin 1964
The first thing that one notices about Wolf Meyer-Christian's design is the style of drawing, which has a subtle elegance unusual for its time. However, Meyer-Christian has been influential not only in methods of representation but also in principles of composition, as shown by Leon Krier's yacht club design opposite. The subdivision of the masses of the building, which is nonetheless clearly defined in totality, the characteristic glass oriels and the system of walkways and ramps all reveal Krier's debt to Meyer-Christian. However, while Krier's work tends towards the monumental, Meyer-Christian's is distinctly subversive. The glass roof of a house sunk into the valley has a two-lane highway thundering over it. The divided walkway crossing the complex destroys not only the formality of the composition but also, because it is disfunctional, the observer's sense of reality. The use of brick in the wall around the housing runs contrary to the monumentality of the design and represents a tendency towards the fictitious which is reinforced by the over-steep stairs, megalomaniacally large halls and roofs alluding to highways. However, this fiction is not meaningless architectural poetry: it uses irony to communicate the antagonism between the artistic motives of the architect and the technical realities of the brief.

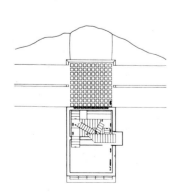
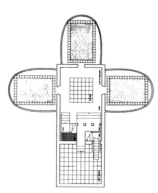
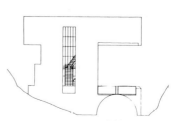

PLANS AND SECTIONS

36

LEON KRIER

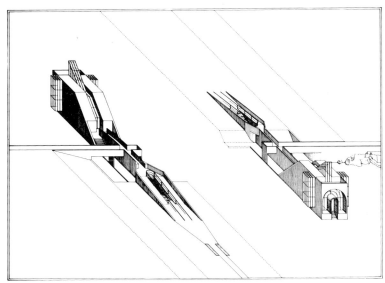

DESIGN FOR A SAILING CLUB

Design for a Yacht Club, 1967
This early design by Leon Krier is in some ways a bridge between Wolf Meyer-Christian's housing project and his brother Rob Krier's first built scheme, the Siemer house.

Here, Leon Krier pushes even further than Meyer-Christian the perfection of the well-considered line. In his isometrics he creates a model-like architecture which appears to hover in a topographical and atmospheric vacuum.

The theme of the design, the 'building on water' was only one aspect of *genius loci* that

Krier tackled while studying under O M Ungers in Berlin.

Centri Rionali Project for the 'Roma Interrotta' Exhibition, Rome 1979
Leon Krier's urban planning, like that of his brother Rob, is modelled after the pre-industrial city of the eighteenth or nineteenth century. However, perhaps because his proposals are more radical than Rob Krier's, they remain for the most part unbuilt.

This scheme is based on the traditional divi-

sion of Rome into a multitude of physically small and functionally complex *riones*. 'The continuous vitality of the *riones* and the spontaneous formation of anti-institutional social centres within the quarters replace the cultural sclerosis of institutions such as the church, the *municipio*, the school, or the *casa popolare*' (Krier). Krier's love of the monumental is illustrated by the 'social centres' in each of the quarters, which are built as halls supported by giant pillars.

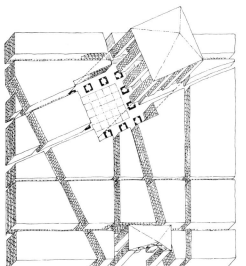
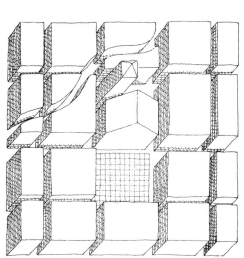
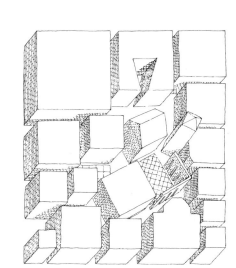

'CENTRI RIONALI', TYPOLOGICAL MODELS OF A CITY QUARTER WITH PROJECTING ISOMETRICS

ROB KRIER

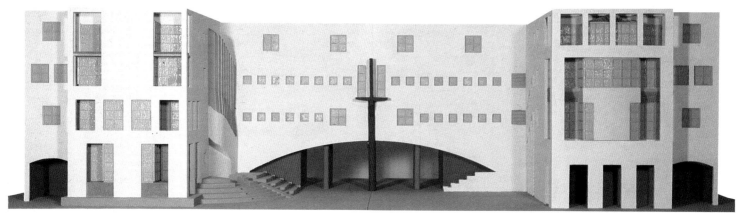

RITTERSTRASSE HOUSING, BERLIN, MODEL

Dwellings on the Ritterstrasse, Berlin 1977-80
These dwellings are part of a block of housing designed by a number of architects in a project for the Berlin International Building Exhibition.

Here, Rob Krier achieves a symmetry not only in the housing but in the street as a whole. The building is an H-shape, and thus appears to have three wings regardless of which way one views it. The central facades on both the outside and the inner courtyard are similar in composition. The forecourt created by the three wings of Krier's building on the street side is mirrored by another building opposite. Both spaces enliven the street and the relationship between the public and the private.

Certain elements in this project are very reminiscent of the housing projects (*Höfe*) of Red Vienna in general, and of Karl Ehn's 'Karl-Marx-Hof' in particular: the shallow curve of the bridge over the central passage, the inverted arrangement of the windows, and the central sculptures underlining the symmetry of the facades. The deep incisions in the trans-

parent framework structure and the glass surfaces are also evocative of buildings by Adolf Loos, such as the 'Loos House' in the Michaelerplatz in Vienna and the house for Tristan Tzara in Paris.

Inside, the arrangement of the space is more characteristic of detached houses than it is of flats, for in some cases Krier has spread the accommodation over several floors, and in others he has extended it from one side of the building to the other. Krier has also transposed a principle of urban planning to the interior by creating a central room around which the other rooms are arranged, as though they were buildings clustered around a public square. This can be seen as evidence of Krier's desire to counteract the uniformity of mass housing with a personalised structure favouring communication and exchange.

Restructuring of the Rennweg, Vienna 1977
The area around the Rennweg was considered the last significant area in need of planning left

within the belt defining the inner city of Vienna.

Krier's plan called for the reinventing and restructuring of the historical fabric of the site. Taking his cue from the *Höfe* in the neighbourhood, he proposed a system of urban blocks containing inner courtyards. By carefully restricting vehicle access, Krier controlled how public, or private, the spaces within the quarter would be. The circulation routes around the quarter were wide open to the public, and connected with underground car parks beneath the blocks for the use of the residents. The central square, however, had no through traffic and was therefore only semi-public. Even more secluded were the courtyards within the blocks, which Krier arranged either as gardens, children's playgrounds, or rest areas for the older residents.

Like the Ritterstrasse dwellings, the Rennweg project was designed to allow a number of different architects to work on the buildings and so create the greatest possible variety of form.

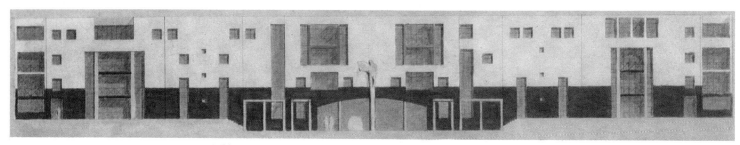

RITTERSTRASSE HOUSING, PROPOSAL FOR ONE OF THE CENTRAL FACADES

RITTERSTRASSE HOUSING, VARIATIONS

BLICK AUS DER SCHLACHTHAUSGASSE

PROJECT FOR THE RESTRUCTURING OF THE RENNWEG AREA, VIEW FROM THE SCHLACHTHAUSGASSE

PETER EISENMAN

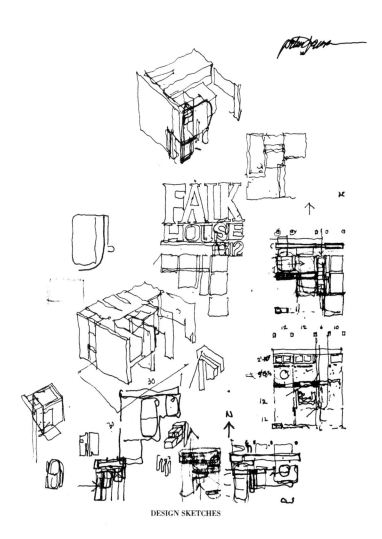

DESIGN SKETCHES

Falk House, Hardwick, Vermont 1969-70
Peter Eisenman is one of the loose-knit 'New York Five', along with Michael Graves, John Hejduk, Richard Meier and the team of Charles Gwathmey and Robert Siegel. What brings the group together is a shared attempt to investigate and reinvest the possibilities offered by the 'heroic' phase of Modernism.

Of all the members of the New York Five, Peter Eisenman makes the broadest claims for architecture: 'Architecture is more than just building . . . for me, architecture is the creation of a meaningful environment'. Consequently, Eisenman uses Modernism not as a pattern book for historical forms, as Richard Meier does with his predilection for Le Corbusier's early work, but as a means of coming to terms with the principles of ordering form in three dimensions. From Modernism Eisenman has inherited a preoccupation with meaningful for-

mal systems and a methodical approach that is particularly evident in the presentation of his projects.

Eisenman calls his house designs – which are numbered consecutively as though they were stages in some scientific experiment – 'cardboard architecture'. Thus it is fitting that the most widely published photographs of the Falk House give the building an appearance much like a cardboard model. The house is above all else a built piece of architectural criticism, the result of a planning process orientated not towards the subject, the users, but towards the object, the problem of architectural form.

Eisenman's objectivity is also reflected in his drawing style. The design sketches, which are called 'planning diagrams' to emphasise their systematic arrangement, are not visually simple perspectives but axonometrics better suited to

the manipulation of the object. These diagrams show how the form-finding process can be set in motion by the rotation and interpenetration of the 'three primary physical systems' – line, plane and volume. This initially results in two superimposed cubes, one defined by columns, the other by walls. A number of so-called stages of transformation are then worked through and when these are put together in a planning diagram, they suggest an order imposed by the object itself: 'I do not believe that I am in control of the objects which I supposedly make,' Eisenman says. It is not really very important whether this order can be justified mathematically or not. Here, not unlike the Mannerists of the sixteenth century, Eisenman is playing a speculative game with the scientifically founded possibilities of representation. In his more recent work, however, he has moved away from this type of planning.

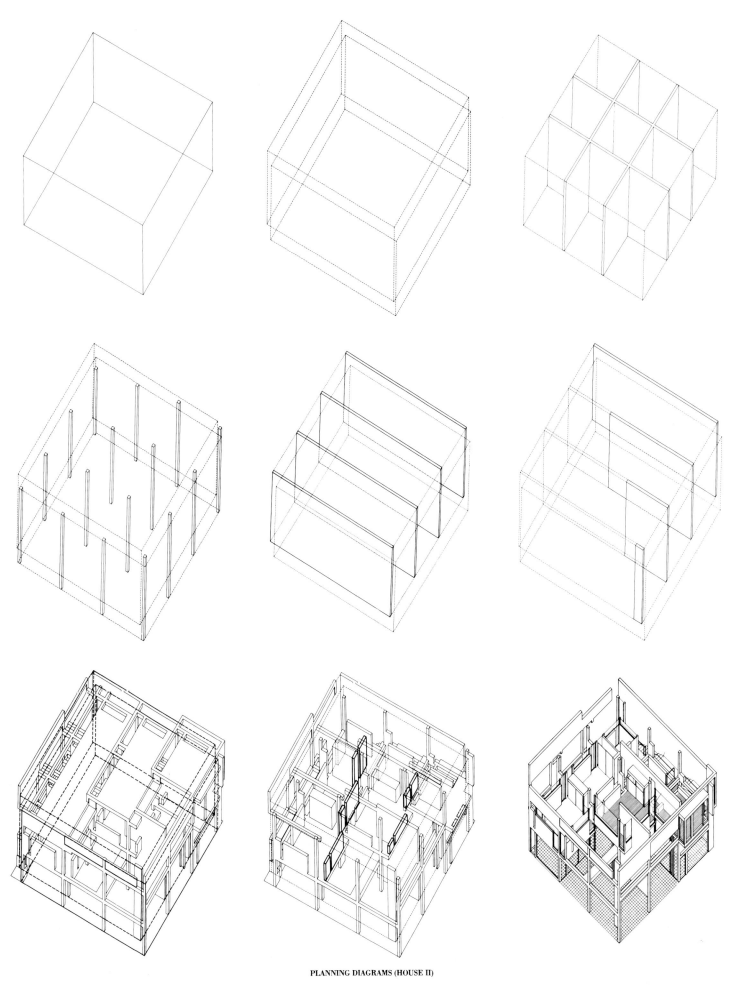

PLANNING DIAGRAMS (HOUSE II)

ADOLFO NATALINI & SUPERSTUDIO

HOUSE ON SAALGASSE, MODEL

Superstudio: *Superstructures*
Towards the end of the sixties programmatic architectural groups were formed all over Western Europe in protest against contemporary industrial society. Amongst the most important of these groups, which combined the disciplines of architecture, design, planning, engineering, painting and photography, were Archigram in England, Haus-Rucker-Co, Coop-Himmelblau and Raimund Abraham in Austria, and Archizoom, Zziggurat, UFO, Studio 65 and Superstudio in Italy.

Superstudio was formed in 1965. Its large photomontages combine the existing architecture of an overflowing civilisation with megastructures of their own making. In the *Il Monumento Continuo* (Continuous Monument) series of 1969, a white superstructure pushes like a glacier from some future ice age through open landscapes and giant cities. In the *Le Dodici Città Ideali* (Twelve Ideal Cities) series two years later, the structure has become a dense grid that stretches as far as the eye can see, dividing up the whole world.
Members: A Natalini, C Toraldo di Francia, R Magris, P Frassinelli and A Magris.

Adolfo Natalini: New House at No 4 Saalgasse, Frankfurt 1980-84
The competition brief which spawned this project had a threefold aim: one, the faithful reconstruction of the traditional half-timbered Römerberg houses in the heart of Frankfurt; two, the construction of a cultural centre for exhibitions, concerts and plays; and three, the provision of new housing in tune with the character of the old neighbourhood.

Natalini designed a new building to stand next to the cultural centre at the end of a row of four houses in the Saalgasse. The building is separated from the others in the row on the left and on the right by pedestrian thoroughfares, and full use is made of the corner site.

The first scheme, illustrated here, divides the house horizontally into seven parts. From the first up to the fourth floor, square windows dominate the facade, dividing it into regular panels. Out of the facade grows a tree, a symbol of the timber used in the traditional houses. This motif reappears in the sketches of the project in the form of bronze branches, which stick out of the corners of the panels and fulfil the very practical function of disguising airintakes.

Natalini has made a contemporary reformulation of the archetypal *Fachwerkhaus*. The result is a changing mixture of reality and fiction which accepts the urbanism that Superstudio rejected so strongly in the sixties.
Collaborators: F Natalini and A Roda.

42

'NEW YORK, NEW YORK' FROM THE CYCLE 'IL MONUMENTO CONTINUO' 1969

'THE FIRST CITY' FROM THE CYCLE 'LE DODICI CITTA IDEALI' 1971

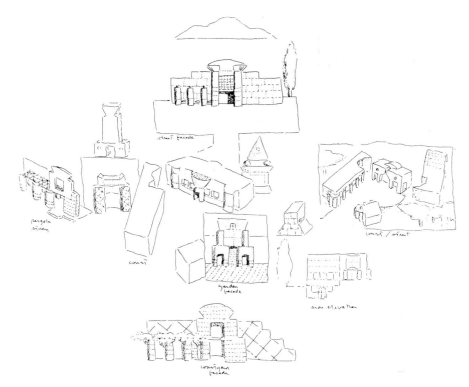

KALKO HOUSE, COMPOSITION SKETCHES, FACADE STUDIES AND ISOMETRICS

KALKO HOUSE, VIEW OF THE LIVING ROOM

MICHAEL GRAVES

PORTLAND BUILDING, PERSPECTIVE VIEW FROM THE PARK

Portland Public Service Building, Portland, Oregon 1980

This was the result of an international competition organised by the city of Portland to design a public building that would 'make a statement', but do so on a restricted budget. The building is sited in the centre of the city next to two classical buildings, the City Hall and the County Courthouse. It has three classical divisions which are clearly in keeping with the symbolic and mimetic qualities of a 'public building': wide plinths at the base, then the mass of the building, followed by a clearly defined top. The base of the building contains public arcades and small shops; the main shaft has offices; and the top is a huge keystone. Graves originally proposed a small group of pavilions for the top – a kind of 'city within the city' comparable to the ancient *agora* or *Forum Romanum* – but this was vetoed by the city authorities and local architects. There were further objections to the decorative flying garlands on the sides, some critics saying that they made the building look like an oversized, berib-

boned Christmas package. In the end, less demonstrative, flat garlands were substituted.

Putting aside the protests, Graves' building is very important because it was the first Post-Modern highrise. And contrary to everyone's expectations of what a highrise should look like, this 20-storey structure is box-shaped. With it, Graves has enlarged the typology of the sky-scraper.

Kalko House, Green Brook, New Jersey 1978

The client laid down two conditions for the design of this house, which is located in the clearing of a densely wooded site which slopes steeply to the back and side, offering a dramatic view towards Manhattan. First, there had to be enough garage space for his sizeable automobile collection. And second, there had to be a large open air swimming pool. The garage and pool project as wings from the central portion of the house in order to engage the positive qualities of the landscape and reinforce the privacy of the site. Nature and building are equated very much in the classical tradition. Moreover, the

design of the house paraphrases certain elements of Raphael's Villa Madama in Rome. One example is the cenotaph-like roof of the central facade, which is framed on axis between eroded pillars.

The Kalko House was the first example of Post-Modernism in Graves' work following his 'Le Corbusier reprises' with the New York Five.

Triptych for the Milan Triennale, 1973

The triptych Graves painted for the Milan Triennale in 1973 demonstrates his fascination with painting not only as a way of extending his architecture, as in a trompe l'œil, but also as an independent means of conveying a message about building and three-dimensionality, architecture and the environment, historical architectural forms and their interpretation.

The milky colours of this triptych are something of a trademark for Michael Graves, for his architecture as well as his furniture and graphics. (*See back cover.*)

45

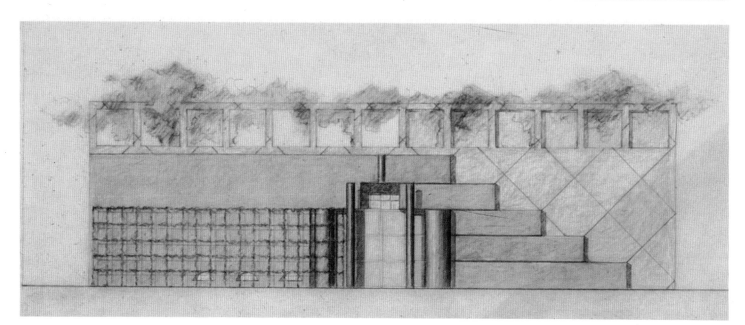

KALKO HOUSE, PRELIMINARY STUDIES AND FIRST PROPOSAL FOR THE STREET SIDE FACADE

PORTLAND BUILDING, COMPETITION MODEL

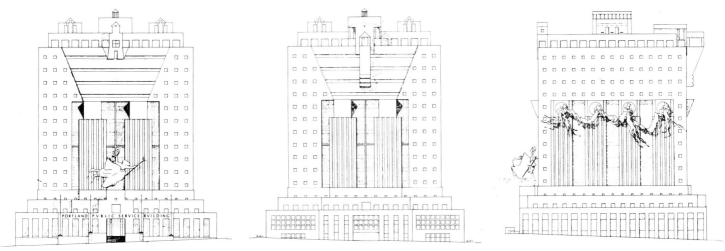

PORTLAND BUILDING, LEFT TO RIGHT: FACADE FROM FIFTH AVENUE, FOURTH AVENUE AND MADISON AVENUE

STEVEN IZENOUR

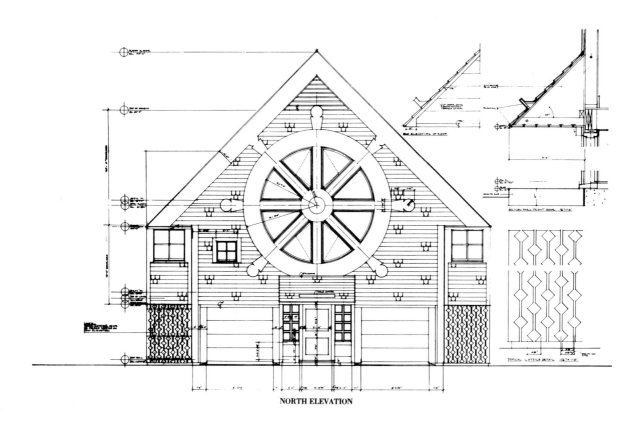

NORTH ELEVATION

**'My Father's House', Long Island Sound
1980-83**

On Long Island Sound, east of New Haven, there are a number of shingle-style houses built between 1850 and 1930. The local vernacular was clearly one source of inspiration for the house Steven Izenour built for his parents. Another was his work in the office of Venturi, Rauch & Scott Brown: in a kind of œdipal opposition to Venturi's 'My Mother's House', Izenour calls this project 'My Father's House'.

The simple, almost square house is dominated by a gable roof similar to those around it. The north, or entrance, elevation is defined by an oversized window shaped like a ship's wheel. This nautical/gothic rosette is flanked on either side by a square window, but in a clear reference to Vanna Venturi's house, Izenour breaks the symmetry and scale of the composition by adding a smaller square window to the left side of the facade. The nautical context of the house is reinforced by a ship's mast with a raised flag and a weather vane as well as by the massive granite jetty on which it stands.

The outer skin of the house is cedar shingle dotted with small, raised cloverleaf patterns. The choice of the cloverleaf motif could be seen not only as a play on the American tradition of 'pattern art', but perhaps also as a reference to idyllic nature.

As in Vanna Venturi's house, the overall symmetrical arrangement of the plan is disrupted by carefully chosen details. The staircase, the entrance hall, the kitchen and the bathroom all appear to be variations of those in 'My Mother's House', and the similarity between the two buildings is even carried through to the pattern of the tiles.

The living room is strongly symmetrical. On axis with the two main windows on the north and south sides is a round table flanked by parallel sofas. When seen from inside, the four Doric columns on the south facade frame the windows and take on the quirky appearance of four sets of gathered curtains. On the opposite wall, there is a Pop Art Doric column which contains the fireplace.

Izenour has brought the shingle-style house up to date. Using modern techniques, regional motifs, nautical symbols, Pop Art, blow-up effects and ironical references to architectural history, he has created a complex, multivalent architecture.

48

SOUTH SECTION

NORTH SECTION

OMA

REM KOOLHAAS AND MADELON VRIESENDORP, 'WELFARE PALACE HOTEL' 1975. PERSPECTIVE VIEW OF COMPLEX

Delirious New York, 1972-76

OMA (Office for Metropolitan Architecture) is headed by the Dutch architect Rem Koolhaas. The name of the group is a play on 'OMU', the nickname of Oswald Mathias Ungers, their teacher, and perhaps also on 'MOMA', the Museum of Modern Art in New York.

The group believes that symbolism, association, fragmentation and collage are the most fruitful avenues of experimentation and observation in the present age, and that the best testing ground for all these things is the large metropolis. In OMA's work, the metropolis is presented as a self-renewing system of anarchistic and traditional symbols (a notion similar to that expressed by Venturi, Scott Brown and Izenour in *Learning from Las Vegas*).

Delirious New York announces the 'second coming' of Manhattanism, an unwritten urban programme that up until the mid thirties made the city a melting pot for different mass-cultures and gave it an almost biological automatism. Manhattan man, they say, is determined and defined not by nature, which he sees

as alien, but by the city, through architecture and urban planning, advertising and cinema, design and art.

The *Welfare Palace Hotel* is part of a larger project, *New Welfare Island*. It consists of six highrises and a horizontal 'waterscraper'. The southern facade of the hotel is the dominant elevation. Three-dimensional fragments have dislocated themselves from the main slab to lead their own lives. The fragments have a double function: separately, they provide small palatial skyscrapers that can be reserved for private functions; together, they form a decorative relief with an explicit figurative message – a city collapsing.

Madelon Vriesendorp's *Dream of Liberty* evokes the death agony of the metropolis. A nuclear war appears to have destroyed the earth: one hemisphere is experiencing a new ice age, the other is a desert wasteland bombarded by lightning. Man is no longer present on the earth. The only reminders of his existence are the ruined artefacts of his culture and civilisation: the sphinx and the pyramids are still

standing like ancient, mythical skyscrapers in the sands, and the Chrysler Building rises above the ice, although its top has broken off and fallen to the ground. Emerging from the Chrysler Building, where she has been imprisoned, is the Statue of Liberty, grown in size and made out of brick. Like a new Prometheus, she is attempting to hold up the 'flame of liberty' and free herself from a civilisation that has fallen into ruin. Another interpretation of the painting makes it a metaphor for the emancipation of woman (the Statue of Liberty) from man (the phallic skyscraper). Skyscraper-men lie defeated all around but they can take consolation, however, in the presence of the sphinx, symbol of male and female union.

The combination of anguish, optimism and individualism in *Delirious New York* have made it something of a bible for young people in creative professions all over Europe and America.
Members: Rem Koolhaas, Elia Zenghelis (founding members); Madelon Vriesendorp, Zoe Zenghelis.

50

MADELON VRIESENDORP, 'DREAM OF LIBERTY' 1974

ALDO ROSSI

STUDENT RESIDENCE IN CHIETI, PERSPECTIVE VIEW

Memorial to the Resistance and Town Hall Square, Segrate 1965
The memorial to the partisans who fought in the second world war is a fountain composed of primary geometric forms – a cylinder on a square base, a rectangle and a triangle. The cylinder houses machinery for the fountain, the rectangle contains a speaker's tribune, and the triangular concrete structure acts to tie them both together: 'The geometrical appearance of much of my architecture is very closely connected to the fact that I was obsessed by the triangle in my years at the Milan Politecnico, where topography was still taught . . . For me, the triangle is the Holy Trinity, it is Professor Gavinelli who taught topography at the Milan Politecnico, it is a whole cluster of things.' The square in which the memorial stands is separated from the surrounding buildings by a wall. Two sides of the square are also marked by column stumps which allude to other possible 'boundaries' of the square.

Scandicci Town Hall, 1972
Like the memorial at Segrate, this competition design is based on the principle of combining primary geometric forms. However, Rossi's geometric minimalism – in contrast to, say, Richard Serra's minimal art – expresses a surreal poetry. He views geometry not as the rational factor ordering a chaotic reality, but as a universal law that has been at the root of all architectural forms throughout the history of Western architecture.

Student Residence in Chieti, 1976
Rossi's design for this competition (in which Giorgio Grassi also took part) has at its centre a communal building which consciously takes up elements of a factory building – a play on the link between study and the social and economic realities of the outside world. Around the central building are grouped the students' flats which, with their wood siding and pitched roofs, bring to mind beach houses, or bathing sheds, or even Laugier's primitive hut. Rossi's choice of iconography clearly reflects the realistic nature of his Rationalism.
Collaborators: G Braghieri and A Cantafora.

Modena Cemetery, 1971
Rossi's extension to the Neo-Classical cemetery in Modena, which he has spent more than a decade modifying and reformulating, is perhaps his most significant work. With his 'language of form', he integrates the architecture for the dead with the architecture of the city of the living. 'In April of 1971, on the road to Istanbul between Belgrade and Zagreb, I was involved in a serious auto accident. Perhaps as a result of this incident, the project for the cemetery at Modena was born in the little hospital of Slawonski Brod, and simultaneously, my youth reached its end. I lay in a small, ground floor room near a window through which I looked at the sky and a little garden. Lying nearly immobile, I thought of the past, but sometimes I did not think: I merely gazed at the trees and the sky. This presence of things and of my separation from things – bound up also with the painful awareness of my own bones – brought me back to my childhood. During the following summer, in my study for the project, perhaps only this image and the pain in my bones remained with me: I saw the skeletal structure of the body as a series of fractures to be reassembled. At Slawonski Brod, I had identified death with the morphology of the skeleton and the alterations it could undergo.'
Collaborator: G Braghieri.

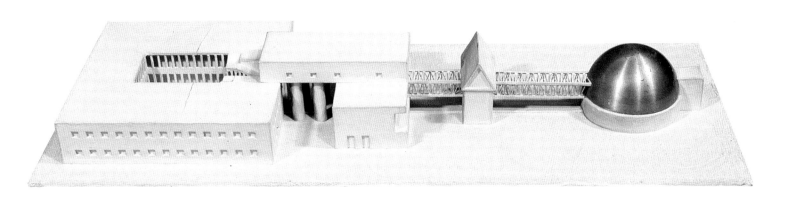

SCANDICCI TOWN HALL, MODEL

STUDENT RESIDENCE IN CHIETI, MODEL

MODENA CEMET[ERY]

TOWN HALL SQUARE AND MEMORIAL IN SEGRATE

54

...EVATION WITH STATUE

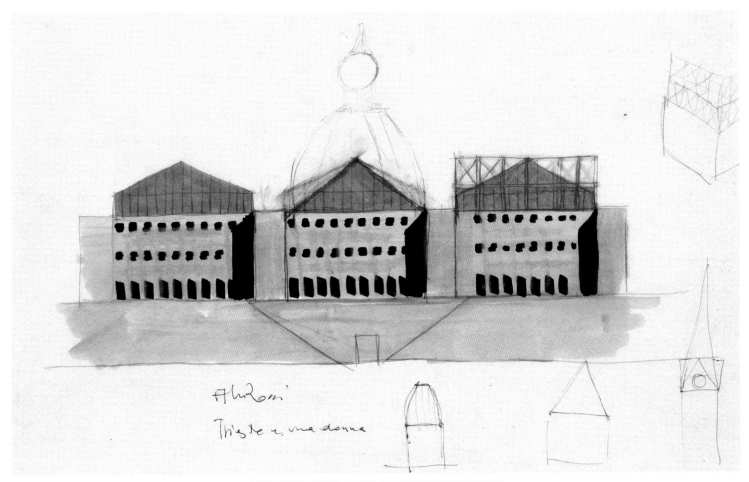

SCANDICCI TOWN HALL, DESIGN ALTERNATIVE WITH DOME MOTIF

MASSIMO SCOLARI

'RECINTO URBANO' 1979

Projects for the 1980 Venice Biennale and 1979 'Roma Interrotta' Exhibition
Massimo Scolari's escape from functional architecture to 'free' pictorial imagery is made plausible by his aphorism: 'Beautiful things are the only friends who never deceive you'. This resigned evaluation of contemporary society also explains, to some extent, the *concetto* at the root of his pictorial inventions.

Porta per città di mare was Scolari's project for the architectural section of the 1980 Venice Biennale. In the catalogue of the exhibition he describes it as a representation of the axonometric picture, and then douses any remaining suspicion that it might actually be buildable architecture by adding: 'This facade could

only conceal its own pictorial image'. Scolari is aware of the contradiction inherent in expressing architectural form and content solely in the medium of art, but unlike Eisenman and Hejduk, he does not draw to depict architectural utopias – his drawings are purely art for art's sake.

In *Porta per città di mare*, the gateway appears as a false perspective in an otherwise conventional landscape. Its warship-like form stands in direct opposition to the shimmering white primitive hut that it frames. The painting poses a problem for the viewer: is he inside the warship-like gate, with his back to a city of similarly threatening architecture, or is he outside the city of his dreams, with the gate preventing him from entering?

In some ways, Scolari's work shows a great affinity with that of Leon Krier. However, while both men share certain basic ideas about the role of architecture in an inhuman environment, the scale of their work is very different. While Krier tackles the reconstruction of entire cities, Scolari is concerned with individual buildings or monuments that at the most can be put into a village context, like the 'recinto urbano', his project for the 'Roma Interrotta' exhibition in Rome in 1979. (It is interesting also to compare the flying machines that often appear in the two architects' drawings. While Krier's are characteristically from the arsenal of the early industrial revolution, Scolari's derive from an atavistic technology.)

56

'PORTA PER CITTÀ DI MARE' 1979-82

THOMAS GORDON SMITH

LONG HOUSE, VIEW FROM THE SOUTH, SECOND PROPOSAL

Long House, Carson City, Nevada 1977-79
Few other Post-Modern architects have pursued the revival of the vocabulary of Classicism with such determination as Thomas Gordon Smith. However, Smith is not an historicist in the manner of Quinlan Terry, who follows the historical pattern stone for stone. On the contrary, he manipulates the elements of classical architecture with a total lack of restraint, and uses contemporary materials and techniques. With some wit, and a fair measure of irony, Smith also applies the alienated and enfeebled symbols of architectural history to buildings which are not normally monumental – the middle-class suburban house and the country villa.

The Long House clearly demonstrates the tense relationship between the historical models and contemporary materials in Smith's work. It is composed of a number of pavilion-like units grouped together around an oval terrace, which opens to the south with views of the surrounding countryside. On a practical level,

the clustering forms a barrier against the sand and wind and creates a sheltered and peaceful environment within. On a theoretical plane, it also represents a clear break with the Modernist convention of a rigidly rectangular building form containing open and flexible space. Here, in place of the relatively neutral shell allowing a variety of uses, there is a variety of exterior forms, with the interior functions being relatively fixed. The polygonal floor plan is reminiscent of those of Baroque hôtels in France, with its anterooms and large rooms for entertaining.

The confrontation between the everyday and the profane in Smith's work recalls both Pop Art and the beginnings of the Californian 'Bay Area Houses', whose architects, such as Bernard Maybeck, took great pleasure in stylistic confrontation and in exaggeration.

Tuscan House and Laurentian House, Livermore, California 1979
These two buildings are named after villas described in Pliny's letters. However, they are in

no way exact reconstructions but rather free and associative interpretations of the ancient types. In their layout and proportions, they hardly differ from the average American suburban houses around them, but their brightly coloured walls are covered with historical references. They are quintessentially what Robert Venturi would call 'decorated sheds'. A massive ellipse and a fragmented portico bring monumentality to the entranceways. Columns and tympana transform the garages into temples. A bare tree trunk is used as a column in a reference not only to the supposed origins of the classical orders but also to the gigantic tree trunk columns in Bernard Maybeck's projects.

In these houses, the deliberately significant collides with the deliberately banal. This is Smith's way of attempting to propagate a kind of timeless storehouse of architectural motifs free from the ideological patina of history and available for new interpretations.

58

TUSCAN HOUSE AND LAURENTIAN HOUSE, VIEWS AND SECTIONS

ETTORE SOTTSASS

'WALKING CITY, STANDING STILL'

The Future of Architecture, 1973
Ettore Sottsass grew up very much in the tradition of early Modernism, for his father was a pupil of Otto Wagner. Since the late fifties, however, he has distanced himself from the maxims of purely functional design, particularly with his work for Olivetti, and since the mid sixties he has been a powerful force behind such motors of design change as Studio Alchimia and Memphis. Sottsass postulates that the worlds of work and play are inseparable, and his designs are correspondingly playful, original, ironic and sometimes cynical.

In 1973, Sottsass produced a series of Pop Art lithographs in which he shot down some well-worn architectural concepts. His favourite targets were the utopians who believed in the linearity of technical progress: in his drawings,

time and nature conquer all their schemes.

Archigram's famous 'walking city' appears to have ground to a halt in a world where nothing – least of all a machine – functions. In the background, tilting skyscrapers sink slowly with time into the sand – a motif also used by Madelon Vriesendorp in her paintings with OMA.

The 'city on tracks', likewise a popular concept among utopian architects of the sixties, is depicted as a millipede trailing wearily over mountains and valleys, its life-support system squeezed out of shape like an empty tube of toothpaste.

In *Architecture-Scooter*, a desolate wasteland is covered as far as the eye can see with an overhead power net. Connected to it like bumper cars are houses that combine the characteristics of an inflatable Moroccan king's tent and a life belt.

In another lithograph, *Architecture-Fleet*, a brightly coloured, inflatable architectural flotilla sails down river in an open, natural landscape. Industrial civilisation has long since collapsed, taking with it all the serious, standardised architecture, and now only humorous carnival buildings decorated with bunting and streamers seem appropriate.

In *Amphitheatre, landed*, a fragmented amphitheatre appears to have crashed like a meteor into the Grand Canyon. It represents *panem et circenses* for a disillusioned public that sees the built environment as something like a sarcastic farce.

Looking back from some distant point in the future, our twentieth-century concepts of architecture seems as strange as objects from outer space.

60

'AMPHITHEATRE, LANDED'

'ARCHITECTURE-FLEET'

'CITY ON TRACKS, SACKED'

'ARCHITECTURE-SCOOTER'

STANLEY TIGERMAN

VILLA PROEH, MODEL

Villa Proeh, Highland Park, Illinois 1979-80
This hill-top villa is immediately distinguishable by the carved-away horizontal masses which step upwards to determine its overall shape. In plan, the building is strongly symmetrical. The entrance has a semi-circular dormer window with a semi-circular glass roof which extends to the rear, where it ends in a triangular gable. At the front of the house, the side wings are subservient to the grand gesture of the entry court, but at the rear, they come forward to form a private circular terrace enclosed by a colonnade of classical inspiration. In its relationship to the site, the villa evokes a gentle Classicism. Its design, like that of Raphael's Villa Madama or Da Vignola's Villa Giulia, is based on the Petrarchan concept of a harmony between culture and nature.

In this villa, the vocabulary of Renaissance architecture – rotundas, little temples, external curving staircases, oval rooms – is combined with an almost Baroque arrangement of rooms to create a modern building that clearly illustrates Robert Venturi's dictum of historical complexity. Tigerman's Villa Proeh gives the impression of being an Italian Renaissance building that has met American Pop Art.
Collaborators: Robert Fugman, Deborah Doyle, Polly Hawkins, Elisabeth Rack.

Project for the DOM Administration Building in Brühl, near Cologne 1980
This project is an entry in a competition to design a new administration building for the DOM company.

One of the principle concerns is to bind the existing, rather chaotic buildings with the new construction, thereby giving the complex a new wholeness. This is achieved primarily by placing the old buildings on either side of the axis of the new building, which is rotated about the orthogonal grid of the rest of the site. From afar, the centre appears to be a perfect cube clad in polished pink granite with pink mirrored glass, but closer up, it is obviously split in two. The section facing visitors as they approach up a road lined with stainless steel pergolas is the public arena containing the reception hall, sales departments and product presentation. The section facing the factory is the private arena of accounting, computing, designing, directing and training. In the centre is the circulation zone, with scissor stairs on either side. Between the two parts of the building are lifts which bear – in massive letters – the insignia 'DOM'. As well as advertising the company, the lifts also serve as a security lock, as one has to use them to get from the public to the private area of the building.

There is a progression upwards through the building. The nearer to the top one gets, the more sumptuous the surroundings and the more senior the employees. At the very top is a roof garden with stainless steel pergolas like the ones lining the main axis. In Tigerman's words, this is a 'heavenly garden, where employees can reflect and contemplate on the position of themselves, the company, and the world'. The garden with the pergolas evokes an Arcadian ideal in stark contrast to the monumental emptiness of the plinth out of which the administration building rises like a monolith to some ancient deity. The presentation drawings reinforce this contrast. In them, the initials of the company form an entrance portal which breaks open to reveal a path which seems to lead to a 'better world' raked by light as in a Baroque painting of heaven.

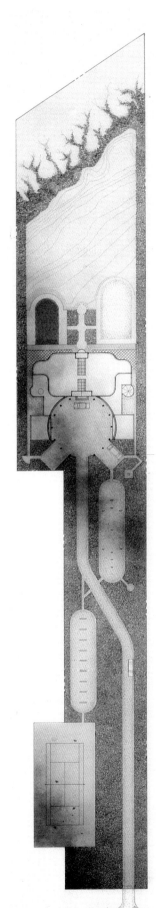

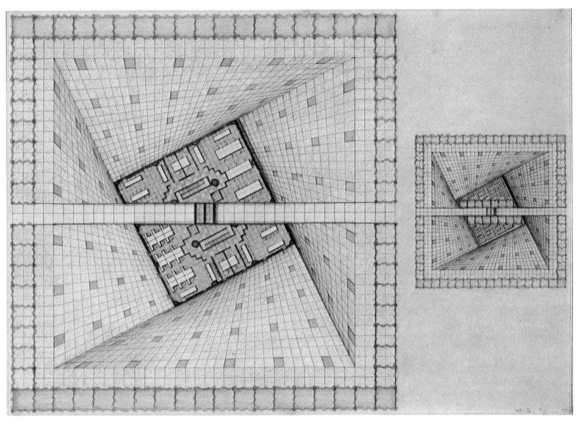

DOM BUILDING, COLOGNE, VIEW UP MAIN ENTRY ACCESS

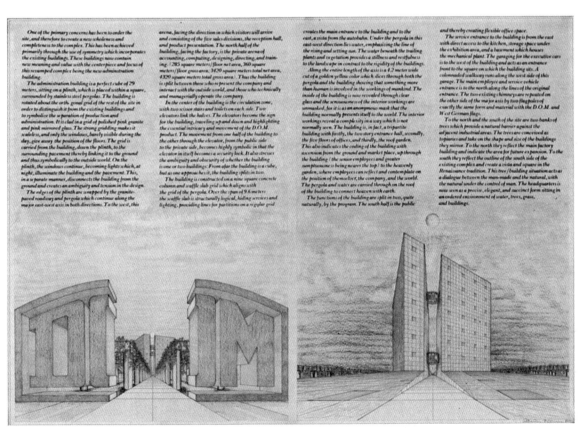

PLANS OF OFFICES AND ROOF GARDEN

63

CHICAGO SEVEN

THE SIX TOWNHOUSE MODELS IN THE MUSEUM'S COLLECTION

Townhouse Competition, Chicago 1978
In 1976, a group of young Chicago designers seeking alternatives to the Miesian traditions of the profession in their city founded the Chicago Seven. By 1978, their number had increased to eleven. That same year, an open competition was held to design a new sort of urban house for Chicago, partly to dispel the notion that the architecture of the city was composed entirely of orthodox Modern skyscrapers. The townhouse was chosen as the basic type for the competition because it was best suited to the gridiron of the city.

The competition, which attracted 169 entries, successfully opened up new perspectives on architecture and town planning. It created conditions favourable for the reintroduction of

historical perspective into contemporary architecture. For the first time in the United States, it was seen that the language of Post-Modernism could effectively confront the realities of the large city.

The models of the Chicago Seven demonstrate a desire not only to reformulate the archetypal urban house but also to restore to architecture in general the status of a public art which must constantly reformulate the relationship between what has already been realised, what has yet to be realised, and what cannot be realised.

Placed side by side, the Chicago Seven's models form a conceptual street: standing on their own, the intricacies of each project are revealed. From left to right, the models shown

are: Stanley Tigerman, five thin slices of concrete alternate solids and voids 'according to the principle of meditation of *yin* and *yang*' with a severe minimalism not at all characteristic of his built work; Stuart Cohen plays on architectural traditions taken from both history and orthodox Modernism – and, in the land of the curtain wall, permits himself a facade without any windows; Frederick Read also juxtaposes different architectural languages but without the implied monumentality of many of the others; Peter Pran's model is a homage to the 'heroic' period of Modernism; Anders Nerheim's is punctuated with geometric cubes and prisms; and Thomas Beeby combines the Palladian ideal of beauty with a far from classical spatial complexity.

PETER PRAN, TOWNHOUSE MODEL

THOMAS BEEBY, TOWNHOUSE MODEL

BERNHARD SCHNEIDER

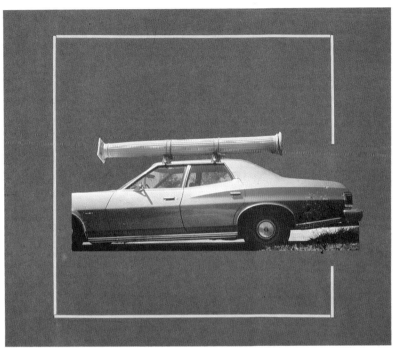

'THE REINTRODUCTION OF THE COLUMN', 1980

The Reintroduction of the Column

In 1975, Bernhard Schneider and Alessandro Carlini – both lecturers at the Berlin Technical University – collaborated on a manifesto entitled *A Plaidoyer for the Reintroduction of the Column*. This was in fact a sarcastic protest against the re-use of the 'antiquated' associations of the column in new, historicising buildings, against the 'brazen familiarity with which this outgoing century is latching onto history again'. In hundreds of small sketches, they created endless trivial variations on the standard columnar orders. Bases, capitals and shafts became bottles of schnaps, women's legs or cigarette butts in a style clearly indebted to Dadaism, Surrealism and Pop Art.

The photomontage reproduced here is a later work on the same theme. It shows a classical column tied up like a suitcase on top of a car luggage rack. The horizontal position and mobility of the column give it the appearance of

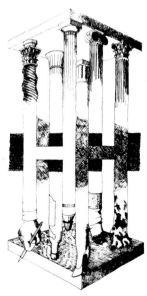

'COLUMNS', 1980

a powerful canon, but also imply that the columnar orders have become transplantable, movable.

Columns, 1980, is a trick picture in the tradition of M C Escher, for it can be turned on its head so that the floor becomes the ceiling and the bases turn into capitals. At one end of the columns are 'classical' capitals, and at the other are 'pop' capitals composed of such things as a feline paw, a pencil or a high-heeled shoe. Thus the revered forms of Classicism are replaced by the debris of contemporary civilisation – an ironic apotheosis.

For Schneider, banning the column was not a step in the historical and cultural continuum but rather a complete break with the past. Correspondingly, his work does not attempt to circumvent the break: it illustrates instead, in his words, 'the change in function of architecture from universal model to entertainment'.

65

JOHN HEJDUK

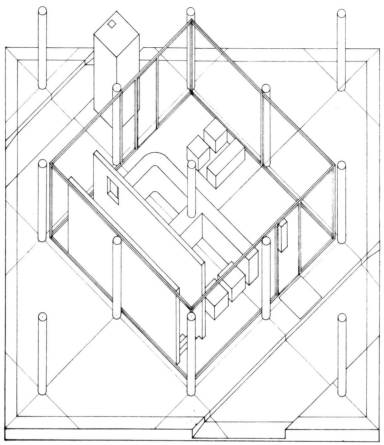

HOUSE A, ISOMETRIC OF THE GROUND FLOOR WITH ENTRANCE AREA

Diamond House Project, House A, 1980
John Hejduk's Diamond Houses are easiest to understand in the context of his teaching at the Cooper Union School in New York, for they are a means of communicating to new students his central thesis on the principles of architectural form. By systematically posing a series of didactic problems, Hejduk attempts to show that the structure of architectural form does not result from an abstract division of space but rather from a modulation of elementary signs.

The first step he takes in elaborating his theory, which owes much to the De Stijl movement, is to discard all the 'ideological baggage' of the Constructivist avant-garde because only one thing interests him, namely, the *poetics* of the autonomous sign. Hejduk demonstrates that he takes the term 'poetics' literally by his description of the elements of the language of architecture: '. . . the mysteries of central-peripheral-frontal-oblique-concavity-convexity . . . the arguments of two-dimensional and one-

dimensional space . . . the ideas of configuration, the static with the dynamic, all begin to take on the form of a vocabulary'. Thus one can see Hejduk's architectural projects, which mostly take the form of drawings, as an attempt to discover the enigmatic syntax of this language.

The Diamond House Project represents the second stage of development in his theory of signs, or design, for it deals with the 'nine-square-grid-problem' of clarifying the division of the (floor plan) surfaces. In the Diamond Houses, the surfaces are set in motion and subjected to stereomatic principles of rotation.

Hejduk is even more insistent on the autonomy of the architectural drawing vis-à-vis the built project than is Peter Eisenman, whose planning diagrams are outwardly similar. And while Eisenman often finds people to build his 'cardboard architecture', Hejduk feels that he need not compromise his drawings by translating them into buildings that have to accommo-

date the needs of their users. Given this fact, it almost goes without saying that Hejduk does not use central perspectives which relate to the subject but isometrics which are orientated to the reality of the object.

The rejection of the central perspective as obsolete also led the architect to the image which gave the Diamond House Project its name: 'The quality of space is conveyed to the observer in the diamond isometrics without using the antique and outmoded form of perspective projection'. This approach, with the radical neglect of the observer that it entails, has led one critic, Frank Werner, to speak of 'neurotic formalism', and another, Raphael Moneo, to compare Hejduk to Copernicus – a presumptious parallel if one knows history well, but one that is justified in that both men take away the finite space which guarantees people their security.

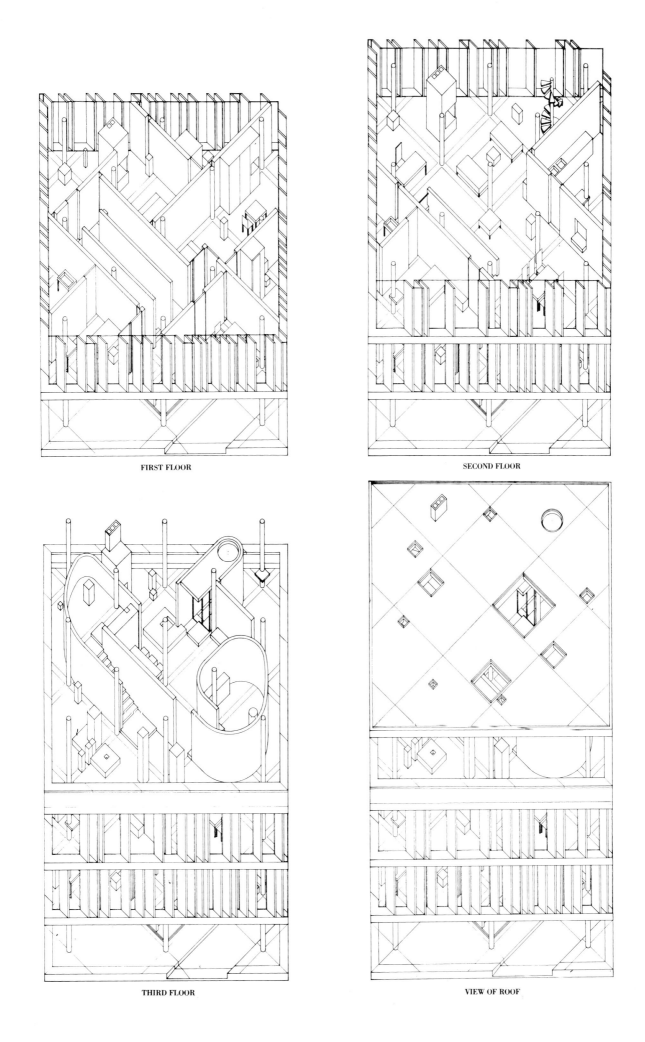

FIRST FLOOR

SECOND FLOOR

THIRD FLOOR

VIEW OF ROOF

HANS HOLLEIN

Early Work
In the early sixties, some time before he had a project built, Hans Hollein worked on a series of collages which showed images of different cities. These can be seen as the first indication of Hollein's interest in the semantics of architecture.

Schullin Jeweller's Shop, Vienna 1974
Hollein's first built work was a small candle shop

with a fragmented facade. Here, this motif reappears in an even more dramatic form. The smooth granite facade is eroded away to reveal almost geological layers of glittering metal, which in turn frame gleaming projecting pipes.

Travel Bureaux, Vienna 1976-79
The isometrics overleaf show two of Hollein's most important travel bureaux. The interiors

evoke multiple associations of travel. The palm trees are an obvious reference to holidays and faraway desert islands. Other signs are the Egyptian pyramids and aeroplane wings.

Kulturforum, Berlin-Tiergarten, 1983-87
Hollein's proposal for the cultural centre of the city of West Berlin will tie together existing building of different character.

'CITY FORMAT

ER VIENNA' 1960

69

BERLIN KULTURFORUM, VIEW OF THE MEETING HALL AND BOW BUILDING

BERLIN KULTURFORUM, PAVILION BUILDING

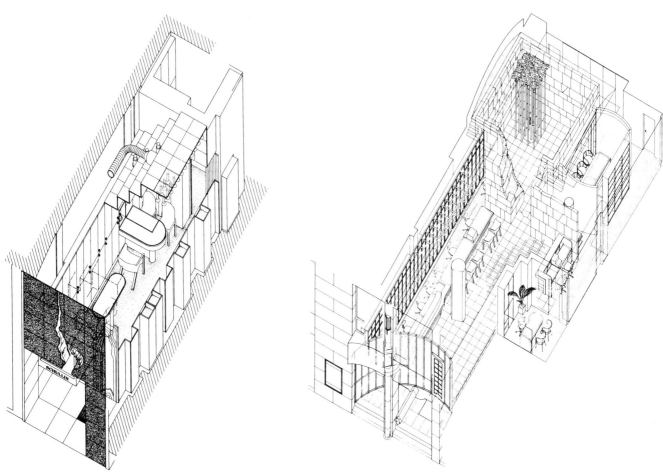

SCHULLIN JEWELLER'S SHOP, VIENNA, ISOMETRIC

AUSTRIAN TRAVEL BUREAU IN VIENNA, STEPHANSPLATZ BRANCH, ISOMETRIC

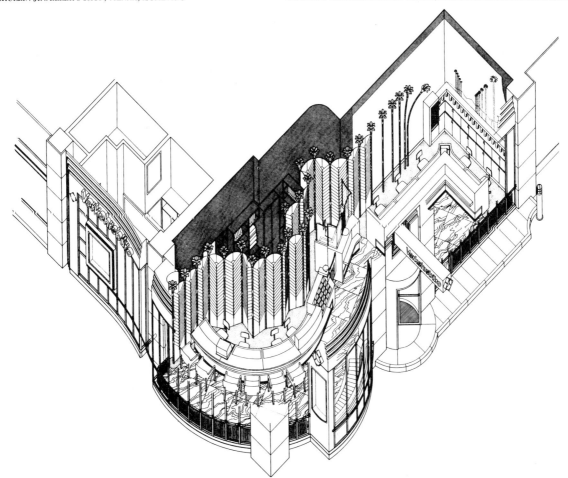

AUSTRIAN TRAVEL BUREAU IN VIENNA, RINGTURM BRANCH, ISOMETRIC

OSWALD MATHIAS UNGERS

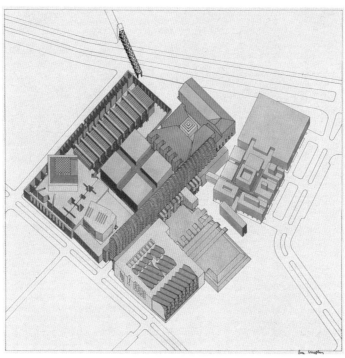

MUSEUM COMPLEX, BERLIN, ISOMETRIC

Housing in the Historic Centre of Marburg 1976

Oswald Mathias Ungers' project for the medieval centre of the hill town of Marburg was concurrent with the revival of 'urban reconstruction' and 'combining new build with old' as themes worthy of an architect's consideration.

Marburg was fortunate in having as a resident Heinrich Klotz, who wished to see the town spared the ravages of either uncompromisingly Modern architecture or pastiche attempts to imitate the traditional half-timbered buildings. He persuaded the authorities of the small town to hire three very well-known architects: Charles Moore was asked to design an apartment complex, James Stirling was given the task of converting an historically important building, and O M Ungers was assigned new housing in a central area encompassing the historic market place, castle and so-called *Steineres Haus*, the oldest secular stone building in the town. Given the context, it would have been easy for Ungers to merely imitate the surrounding buildings: instead, he demonstrated his creativity by outlining a wide variety of possible solutions which incorporated different architectural typologies.

Ungers finally chose to build five tall, narrow houses next to the *Steineres Haus*, each with its own distinctive character, but each part of a 'diversified whole'. The different house types draw strongly on elements of the local vernacular, such as corbelling, half-timbering and exterior stairs, but Ungers did not intend this to be merely a play on historical forms. Rather, it is the basis of an architectural vocabulary which is open to interpretation as it undergoes a process of transformation. The treatment of the stairs clearly illustrates this idea. Depending on the house, the stairwell can be either isolated or integrated, elliptical in form or symmetrical, only one flight high or several.

The typology of these houses is so specific to Marburg that it is almost impossible to imagine them transposed onto any other town. Ungers is clearly not part of the Modernist body of thought which attempts to solve every architectural problem with a prototype applicable to all places and circumstances.

Collaborators: H Kollhoff, Th Will and K L Dietzsch.

State Museums, Berlin-Tiergarten 1965

The competition brief for a museum complex for the federal state of Prussia called for an art library, accommodation for a collection of paintings and antiques, a copper-engraving facility and a museum for arts and crafts. The site was an open space defined by three important but very different buildings: Mies van der Rohe's National Gallery, Von Stüler's Church of St Matthew and Scharoun's Philharmonic.

Ungers used the analogy between the disunity of the surrounding buildings and the multiplicity of the museum programme as the theme of his design, giving each of the buildings in his complex its own solution and individual identity. In doing so, Ungers was taking a stand against the Modernist principle of uniformity, whereby widely different functions are housed within a single neutral shell and thus rendered indistinguishable from one another.

As in a small-scale city, the individual buildings were tied together to form a whole. The backbone of the complex was a glass-covered pedestrian thoroughfare containing not only the entrances to the various museums but also shops. Ungers re-used this motif of a public arcade within a museum in his proposal for the Museum of Modern Art in Frankfurt.

Collaborators: U Flemming and J Sawade.

NEW HOUSING IN MARBURG, ISOMETRICS

RICHARD MEIER

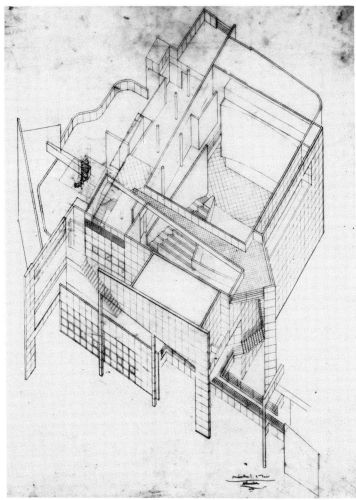

SALTZMAN HOUSE, AXONOMETRIC

Saltzman House in East Hampton, New Jersey 1967-70

The Saltzman House is a rather large weekend retreat for a family with two children. It is divided into two: the larger part contains the family's living quarters, the smaller part serves as a guest house. Such a clear separation of public and private functions, reinforced here by the bridge between them, was a trademark of the New York Five's early houses. The pure geometric form of the building, combined with the transparency of the glazing, demonstrate Meier's respect for the tenets of early Modernism.

The purist membrane of the exterior of the house embraces the rooms in the interior. In the main building, these rooms are centred around a multi-level space and are ordered by slim, round columns which reinforce the ethereal character of the overall composition. Graceful bridges and walkways tie the spaces together.

The central space serves as a dining area on the ground floor and provides a focus for the living room, studio and children's play area above. At the southwest corner of the building is a sun deck. Normally, this is considered an essential part of any weekend house in the area, but here it can also be seen as evocative of the leitmotif of the architecture as a whole – the ocean liner. The allusions to the super-structure of a white 'ocean-going palace' are particularly obvious in the numerous connecting walkways with ship-like handrails. Moreover, Meier takes up the concept of 'Neues Bauen' quite directly in the southeast

corner of the main building, where he very clearly quotes Le Corbusier's Villa Savoye in Poissy. Meier himself denies that the relationship between his work and that of Charles Edouard Jeanneret is overly derivative, and the complexity of his buildings, as shown for example by the tense ordering of the facade, demonstrates that he knows how to develop the ideas of his theoretical master. The combination of Meier's obvious fascination with technology and his choice of the 'ocean liner' motif make the Saltzman House a particularly significant expression of an architect who sees the *esprit nouveau* of the young Le Corbusier shining through the dense rhetoric of Late Modernism.

74

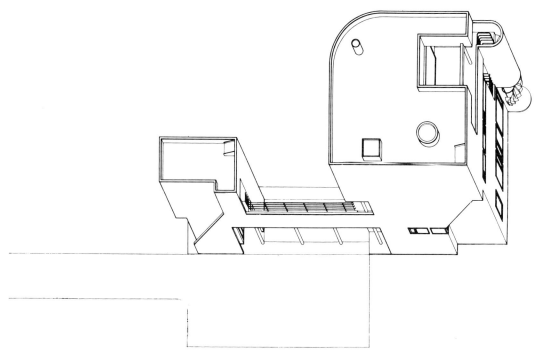

ISOMETRIC FROM THE NORTH

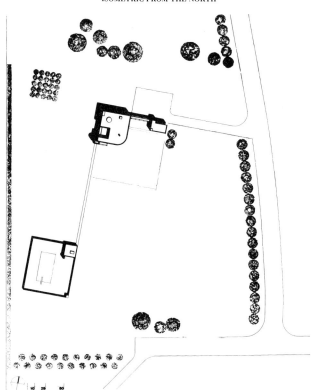

SITE PLAN

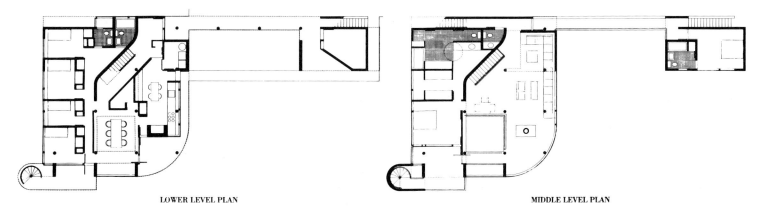

LOWER LEVEL PLAN

MIDDLE LEVEL PLAN

75

ROBERT VENTURI

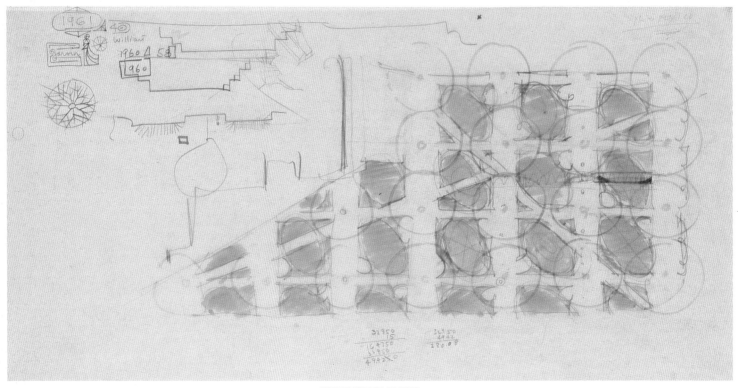

COPLEY SQUARE, BOSTON

Copley Square Competition, Boston 1966
The basic idea of this proposal was to make the park reflect in miniature the street grid of the city around it: to create a microstructure which would make the macrostructure of Boston more comprehensible and habitable. Thus, for example, H H Richardson's Trinity Church, which dominates one side of the square, reappears as a small-scale model in the miniature city plan.

Planting creates the primary grid of regular squares although, as in a real city, the right angles are sometimes sliced through by diagonal paths. The system of diagonal paths was chosen not only because it symbolically undermined the primacy of the right angle but also because it very practically accommodated the natural desire of most pedestrians to find the shortest route from A to B.

By laying out the park as a maze of streets, Venturi is accommodating the individual who would comfortably walk along a street, but feel ill at ease in an open piazza; in short, the average American.
Collaborators: Gerod Clark and Arthur Jones.

'My Mother's House', Chestnut Hill, Pennsylvania 1962
This small house was built in 1962, four years before Robert Venturi's work, *Complexity and Contradiction in Architecture,* was published. It clearly embodies the architectural thought expressed in the book and has had more influence on architecture as a whole than any other house built in the past thirty years.

Access to the site, which is planted with trees and shrubs, is via a road which widens out in front of the main facade to provide space for cars to be parked. A large saddle roof spans the structure in an almost conventional manner and determines the form of the imposing triangular gable. The summit of the gable is pierced by a large slit which, together with the recessed entrance loggia and the central chimney, gives the house an almost Palladian symmetry. The two ends of the main facade determine the functional arrangement of the house: the horizontal bay on the right is balanced by a little square window on the left, near the entrance, which repeats itself, increasing to four times its original size. The concrete lintel above the door

is completed by an arched moulding which is interrupted by the slit on the facade.

The rear facade is also a tensely balanced composition of doors and openings crowned by a balcony – a motif which Venturi reintroduced to modern architectural language. (The first example of its re-use is in the Guild House, Philadelphia, built between 1960 and 1963.)

The plan of the house is a simple rectangle. The rooms are grouped around a core where two vertical elements – the fireplace-chimney and the stair – compete for central position. Venturi has said that this is a 'little house with a big scale', and certainly the elements inside are big: the fireplace seems to be 'too big' and the mantel over it 'too high'. Outside, the big scale is reflected in the main elements, which are large and few in number. The juxtaposition of all these forms, combined with the distortions and complexities in the arrangement of the interior, make this the seminal plan of Post-Modernism.

76

'MY MOTHER'S HOUSE', VIEWS OF THE MODEL

MARIO BOTTA

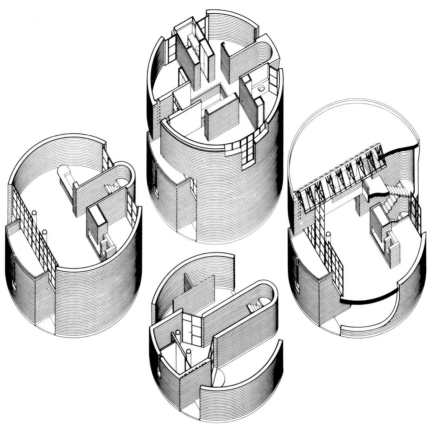

CASA ROTONDA, AXONOMETRICS

Casa Rotonda, Stabio 1980-82

Since 1961 Mario Botta has constructed a series of houses, each of them the realisation of an extraordinary conceptual design, for he has used every opportunity to create new definitions of the traditional family house.

The basic form of the Casa Rotonda is a cylinder. One good reason for this choice was the fact that the rounded, largely closed outer wall deflects the summer sun. The main source of natural light to the stair and upper living area – a glazed slit in the roof – can also be closed off during hot weather to give further protection from the sun.

The cylinder is open on one side to make room for a garden terrace with views out over the valley. On the other side, the outer walls open to express the stair tower. The stair tower becomes a column, with a frieze at the top and a smooth plinth at the base, that symbolically supports the roof.

Inside, the house is surprisingly full of light, although the fenestration is a clear departure from the local vernacular. Botta's Casa Rotonda stands in contrast to nature and to the rest of the buildings around it.

 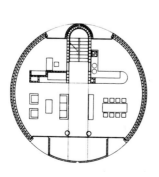 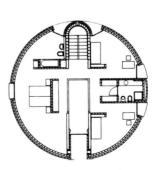 

CASA ROTONDA, FROM LEFT TO RIGHT: SECTION, FIRST LEVEL PLAN, SECOND LEVEL PLAN AND SOUTH ELEVATION

SITE

NOTCH PROJECT, MODEL

Notch Project, Sacramento 1976-77
SITE (Sculpture in the Environment) brings together architects, sculptors, technicians and artists in a group which rates human pragmatism more highly than 'permanent' architectural values. Its projects are commentaries on the mores of our time.

SITE is well known for its work for Best Products, a large catalogue showroom merchandiser. Normally, the retail outlets for this type of organisation are large, windowless, featureless boxes. In the SITE projects, they are transformed.

In Sacramento, the main entranceway is a large, raw-edged gap removed from one corner of the structure. The corresponding positive wedge-shaped unit is mounted on a rail system to open and close the showroom. An internal electric motor and chain drive are located under the steel floorplate. When activated, this mechanised 42-ton 'wandering wall' unit moves 40 feet in either direction, requiring three minutes to open or close the entranceway. When open, the cantilevered second storey and exterior walls are exposed, providing a canopy area which functions as a shopping plaza.

The Notch Project is an ironic commentary on contemporary public art and its token status as a decorative accessory – or what the architectural profession so often refers to as 'integration of the arts'. The Notch Projet suggests integration by retaining the biographical evidence of a disintegration which establishes a new relationship between art and architecture. When the Notch is closed, the showroom exists as a simple warehouse distinguished only by its broken fissure. When open, it becomes both a building and a separate, but obviously related, 'monument'.

Members: James Wines, Alison Sky (founding members); Michelle Stone and Emile Sousa.
Collaborators: Simpson, Stratta and Associates (Architect and Engineer); Allied Engineering and Production Corporation (Engineer for wandering wall).

Text extracted from SITE *by P Restany, B Zevi and SITE, Academy Editions, London*

PEELING PROJECT, RICHMOND, VIRGINIA 1971-72

SUBSCRIBE TO
Architectural Design
+
Art & Design

Architectural Design has for many years been acknowledged as foremost among a small number of publications providing up-to-date information on architecture of the present and past. Each issue tackles in depth a theme of relevance to present-day architectural practice – the work of an important new architect, a currently influential historical figure or movement, or the emergence of a new style or consensus of opinion. The high standard of writing, editorial selection and presentation within Architectural Design has made it one of the world's more progressive architectural magazines and essential reading for anyone interested in the art of architecture.

A subscription to both *Architectural Design* and *Art & Design* will give you twelve issues of *Art & Design* and six double issues of *Architectural Design* annually at a saving of over £20 or $50 off their value if purchased individually. To take advantage of this amazing value- for-money offer, fill in the tear-off form and return it to:

**Subscription Department
AD EDITONS LTD
7-8 Holland Street
London W8
Tel: 01-402 2141**

All major credit cards accepted

ARCHITECTURAL DESIGN + ART & DESIGN

Please send me one year's subscription to both magazines
UK/Eire £45.00 ($75.00 overseas or sterling equiv) Students £39.50 ($65.00 overseas)

☐ **Payment enclosed by cheque/postalorder/draft**

☐ **Please charge my credit card account no:** (all major cards accepted)

Expiry date . . . .

Signature ....

Name ....

Address..

....

....

TO YOUR NEWSAGENT

Please deliver my monthly copy of Art & Design (£1.50)

Signature ....

Name ....

Address..

....

....

**Subscription Department
AD EDITIONS LTD
7-8 Holland Street
LONDON W8**

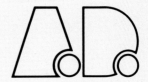

THE ARCHITECTURE MUSEUM

Frankfurt 1979-84

O M UNGERS' BUILDING IS INTENDED TO be not just a backdrop for the German Architecture Museum, but a fine piece of architecture in its own right.

At a time when people are discovering the value of the existing built environment, it makes sense to use an old building as the key element in a new one. The core of the Museum is an historic villa built in 1901. To this, Ungers has added an outer wall which encircles the site like a rusticated 'city wall', keeping out the noise from the traffic roaring along the Schaumainkai and Schweizerstrasse and enclosing the Museum behind it. So that visitors are not put off by this clearly introverted arrangement, the wall opens up on the facade facing the river to make way for an inviting loggia with views right through to the back of the Museum. At the back, the wall goes around a series of small courtyards which are open to the sky. These were built, on the one hand, to give the chestnut and ash trees on the site room to grow, and on the other, to provide small-scale, outdoor settings for the display of architectural objects. Thus, while the surrounding wall has a powerful presence in the environment, it still permits transparency and spatiality.

The area between the outer wall and the old building is covered in glass. This glass enclosure links a front foyer, side passages and a rear hall with an inner courtyard containing a chestnut tree that spreads its branches over the hall. The inner walls of the courtyard form a glass cube divided by a grating into four squares. Here, the proportions and masses permeating the whole of the rear hall are clearly visible; the distances between the columns and even the roof elements are determined by the formal order of the square.

The rear hall is the antipodes of the old house. A great deal of the old building's character comes from the historicising elements on its facade, such as the Ionic columns, the rounded dormer windows, and the rusticated plinths which provided the inspiration for the rustication of the outer wall.

Inside, the old building is surprisingly spa-cious, allowing ample room for a new core – a 'house within a house' – to be inserted vertically through it. However, this structure is only hinted at on the lower levels. On the ground floor all one sees are four freestanding columns resembling a light baldachino. This 'four column room' is ringed by a thin perforated wall. Here Ungers begins to articulate the theme of the architecture: the concept of a succession of rooms and shells one inside the other becomes clear. On the first floor, the main hall has six columns which are arranged so that the room appears to have three naves. In the centre of the hall, the four column room reappears, but in a more solid form. The square motif of the wall on the floor below is taken up again in the open framework which runs around the top of the columns. The four columns define an opening in the ceiling. Looking up, the succession of the rooms becomes clear. One can see – from side on – how the four column room rises through all the upper storeys of the house, getting narrow-er and narrower until it reaches the top, where it turns into the clear symbolic representation of a house with walls and square windows to let in the light. Looking more closely, one becomes aware of a further shell which separates the outer facade of the old building from the main exhibition spaces, creating shafts in between for installations such as a staircase – albeit a narrow one – and a cargo lift. In addition to providing space for the infrastructure of the building, the double wall also serves as an insulator.

Once the structure of the house is under-stood, it becomes clear that Ungers is making a reference to the 'thematics' of architecture. This building is not an abstract container for utilitarian spaces designed only to fulfil certain given functions. Rather, it illustrates a central idea: it tells the story of how the four column room, or baldachino, has evolved into the house. The four column room signifies in gene-ral the roof that offers shelter. And, as Sir John Summerson has shown, the baldachino has al-ways been the architectonic symbol for the centre of the world. By erecting four columns, man defines his identity in the undefined ex-panse of space. The theme is clear. The architecture is the 'signifier' in a representative fiction, relating the evolution of the house in the vertical sequence of spaces, and the sheltering function in the horizontal sequence of shells. The building has an illustrative role, without its aesthetics being reduced to ornamental trimmings.

Ungers belongs to the tradition of the Modern in that he does not use applied ornament. The whiteness of the rooms appears to conform with Bauhaus ideals, and the simplicity of all the architectural elements – the sharp geometric forms, the unornamented restraint – seems to bow to the dogma of the 'Neues Bauen'. Howev-er, the white of these rooms is not the same symbol of purification that Gropius and Le Corbusier strove for, but a white that demater-ialises the space around it. Ungers manages to make us almost forget the material composi-tion of the interior, creating what one might even call a metaphysics of architecture. Only the solid partitions around the displays bring the spaces closer to three-dimensional reality.

This effect vehemently contradicts the char-acter of the rear exhibition hall, where one encounters the material heaviness of the stone everywhere; for example in the ashlar plinths of the old building and the roughly hewn stones of the small courtyards. In contrast to the trans-cendental inner world of the old building what dominates here is the robustness of the outer world, defined by the surrounding 'city wall'. One could say that the ashlar and sandstone facing around the entrance constitute the 'ornament' of this part of the building, because they highlight the heaviness of the stone.

In that Ungers has made architecture speak once more and has clearly characterised the different parts of the building, he is a long way from the traditional concepts of a Modern architecture in whose name the similarity of all parts is demanded. Here, the architecture ac-quires the force of a system of figuration. It goes beyond function to become fiction.

Heinrich Klotz

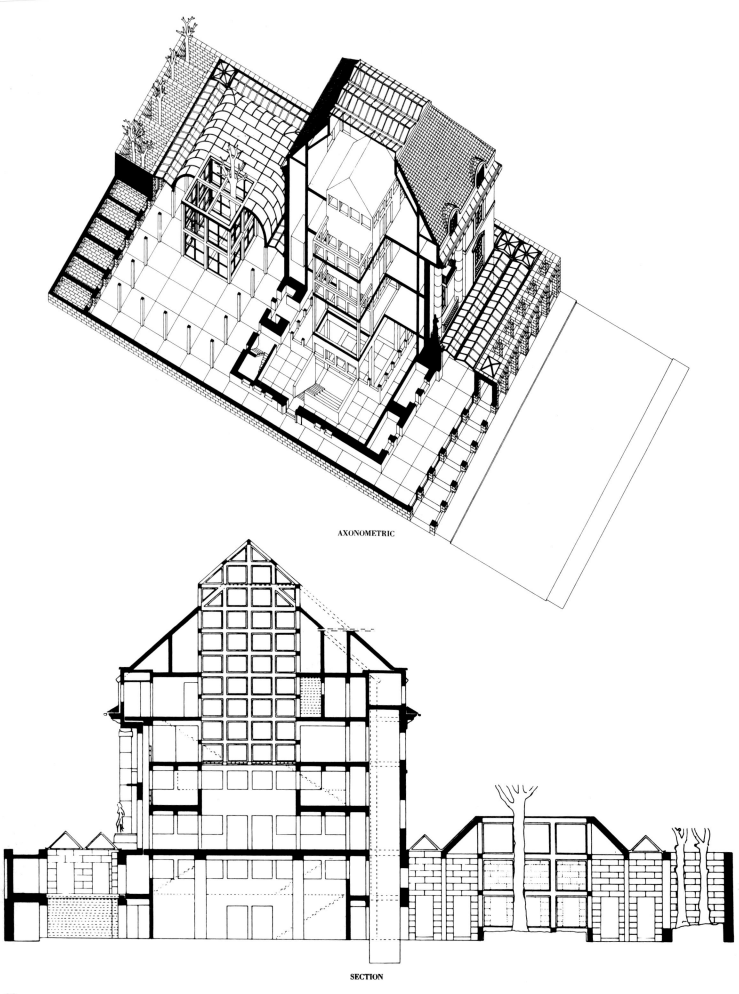

AXONOMETRIC

SECTION

PRELIMINARY SKETCHES

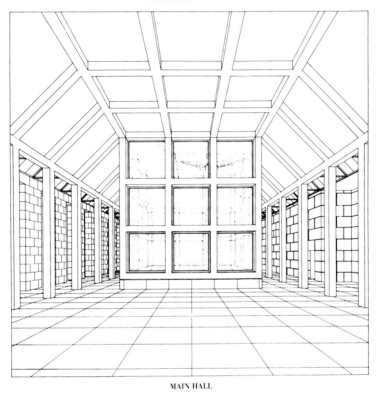

MAIN HALL

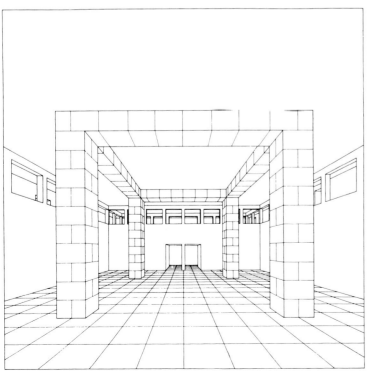

FOUR COLUMN ROOM

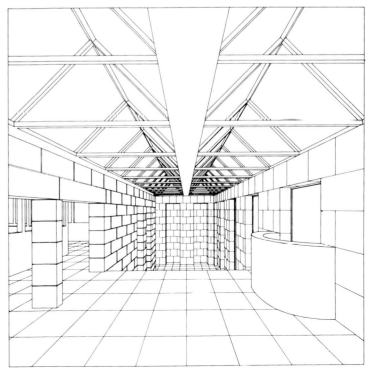

ENTRANCE HALL

SOUTHEAST ELEVATION

SOUTHWEST ELEVATION

NORTHWEST (RIVERFRONT) ELEVATION

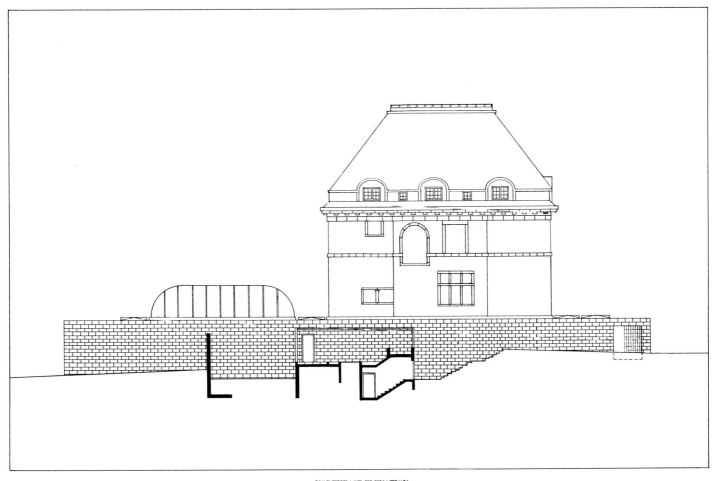

NORTHEAST ELEVATION

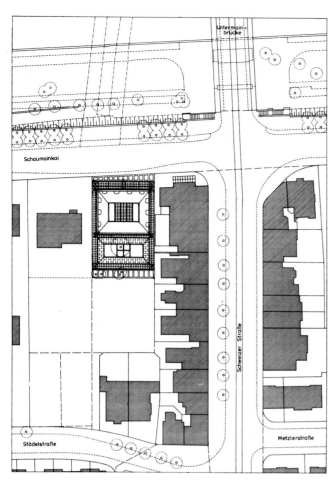

SITE PLAN

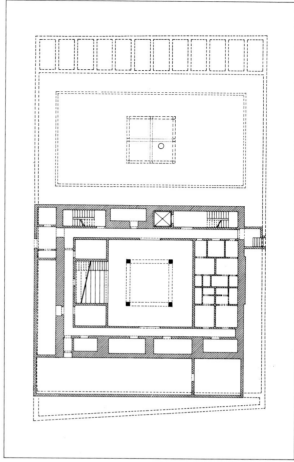

LEVEL ONE

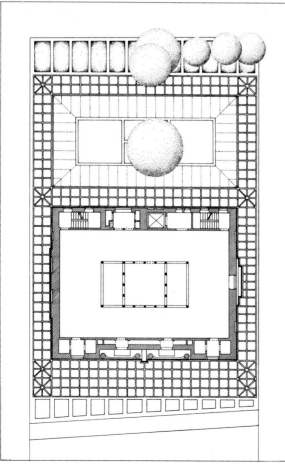

LEVEL FOUR

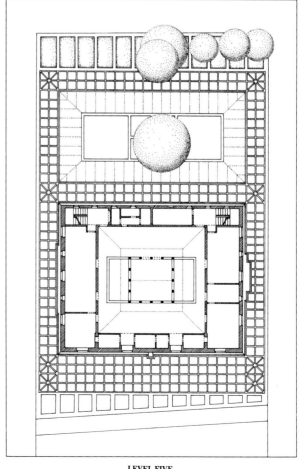

LEVEL FIVE

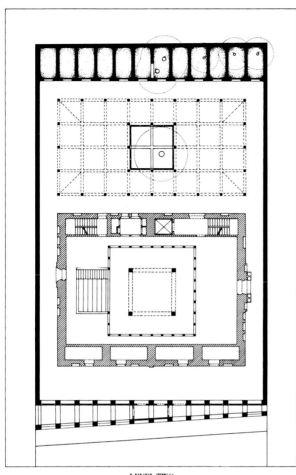

LEVEL TWO

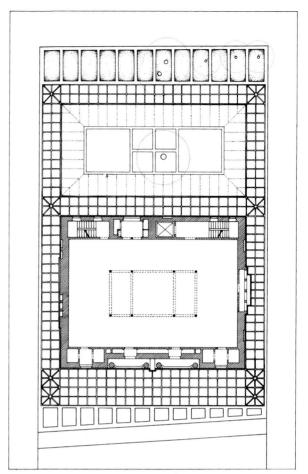

LEVEL THREE

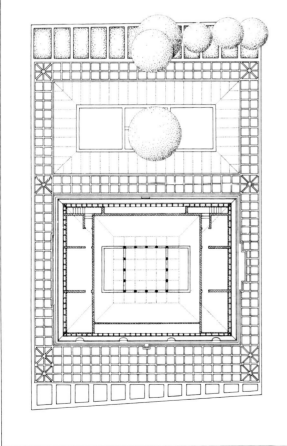
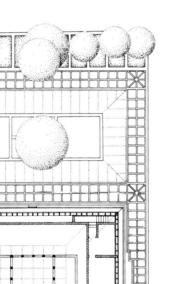

LEVEL SIX

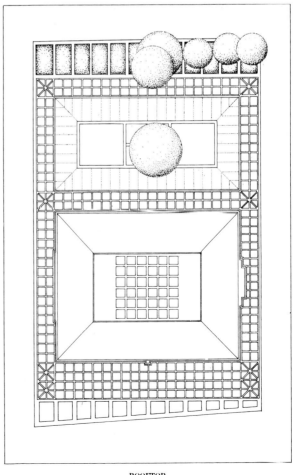

ROOFTOP

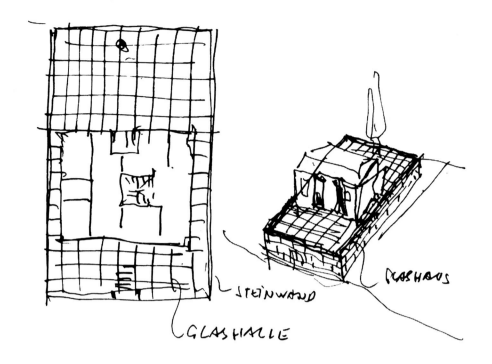

STEINWAND

GLASHALLE

GLASHAUS

ARCHITEKTUR MUSEUM FRANKFORT 2.9.79
1. SKIZZE   O. M. U

CONCEPTUAL SKETCH

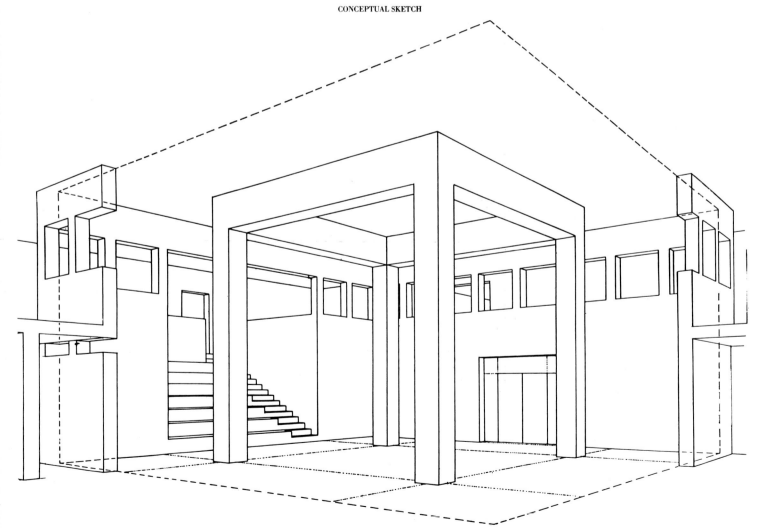

INTERIOR PERSPECTIVE

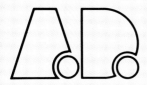

SUBSCRIBE TO
Architectural Design
+
Art & Design

Architectural Design has for many years been acknowledged as foremost among a small number of publications providing up-to-date information on architecture of the present and past. Each issue tackles in depth a theme of relevance to present-day architectural practice – the work of an important new architect, a currently influential historical figure or movement, or the emergence of a new style or consensus of opinion. The high standard of writing, editorial selection and presentation within Architectural Design has made it one of the world's more progressive architectural magazines and essential reading for anyone interested in the art of architecture.

A subscription to both *Architectural Design* and *Art & Design* will give you twelve issues of *Art & Design* and six double issues of *Architectural Design* annually at a saving of over £20 or $50 off their value if purchased individually. To take advantage of this amazing value-for-money offer, fill in the tear-off form and return it to:

**Subscription Department
AD EDITONS LTD
7-8 Holland Street
London W8
Tel: 01-402 2141**

All major credit cards accepted

ARCHITECTURAL DESIGN + ART & DESIGN

Please send me one year's subscription to both magazines
UK/Eire £45.00 ($75.00 overseas or sterling equiv) Students £39.50 ($65.00 overseas)

☐ **Payment enclosed by cheque/postalorder/draft**
☐ **Please charge my credit card account no:** (all major cards accepted)

Expiry date . . . .

Signature ....
Name ....
Address...
....
....

TO YOUR NEWSAGENT

Please deliver my monthly copy of Art & Design (£1.50)

Signature ....
Name ....
Address...
....
....

**Subscription Department
AD EDITIONS LTD
7-8 Holland Street
LONDON W8**

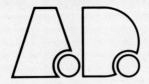

**Subscription Department
AD EDITIONS LTD
7-8 Holland Street
LONDON W8**

TO YOUR NEWSAGENT

SUBSCRIBE TO
Art & Design
with
Architectural Design

Art & Design covers the worlds of art and design with style, in depth, bravely, without bias, with opinion, with understanding, succinctly, with a difference, specifically, questioningly, outspokenly, overtly, with information, with consideration, challengingly, and monthly.

Art & Design is available from newsstands nationally. To reserve your monthly copy, fill in the tear-off form and hand it to your local newsagent. You may also take out a joint subscription to *Art & Design* and *Architectural Design*, which will give you six double issues of *Architectural Design* together with twelve issues of *Art & Design* annually at a saving of over £20 or $50 on their value if purchased individually. To take advantage of this amazing value-for-money offer, fill in the tear-off form and return it to:

ARCHITECTURAL DESIGN + ART & DESIGN

Please send me one year's subscription to both magazines
UK/Eire £45.00 ($75.00 overseas or sterling equiv) Students £39.50 ($65.00 overseas)

☐ **Payment enclosed by cheque/postalorder/draft**
☐ **Please charge my credit card account no:** (all major cards accepted)

[| | | | | | | | | | | | | | | | |] Expiry date . . . .

Signature ....
Name ....
Address..
....
....

**Subscription Department
AD EDITIONS LTD
7-8 Holland Street
London W8
Tel: 01-402 2141**

All major credit cards accepted